YITZHAK RABIN

THE BATTLE FOR PEACE

YITZHAK RABIN

THE BATTLE FOR PEACE

Linda Benedikt

HAUS
BOOKS
London

Originally published in Great Britain in 2005 by
Haus Publishing Limited
26 Cadogan Court
London SW3 3BX
www.hauspublishing.co.uk

A CIP catalogue record for this book
is available from the British Library

ISBN 1-904950-06-X

Designed and typeset by Andrea El-Akshar, Köln

Printed and bound by Graphicom, Vicenza, Italy

Front cover: Getty Images

Back cover: Getty Images

Contents

Introduction

For many Yitzhak Rabin embodied the typical Israeli. Born in British-administered Palestine, he grew up at a time when it became clear that Jewish and Palestinian nationalism would not be able to live side-by-side. As a young man he fought in Israel's war of independence and then spent the rest of his life in the service of his country. Like the emblematic 'sabra', he was a man of action not words, not a man of the book but of the sword. He was an inhibited man, often curt and gruff to cover up his painful shyness, and was admired rather for his analytical skills and intellectual honesty than for his personality. However, he is best remembered and most admired for his political achievement: the Oslo process that was to deliver one of the most desirable ideals in the conflict-ridden Middle East – peace. Yitzhak Rabin was the first Israeli politician to truly break with the tradition of decades of political deadlock, by acknowledging that the Israeli–Palestinian conflict was the cause, not a result, of the wider Arab–Israeli conflict. However, he was unable to overcome his own doubts and suspicions and consequently unable to help his people to overcome theirs; their sometimes carefully-orchestrated but always very real fears, denials and insecurities.

Although his deep-rooted personal inhibitions did not make him a likely candidate for public office, he attained the highest military and political positions the Israeli state has to offer. His primary motivation was the security of his country, for which he was prepared to go a long way. He hated unnecessary chit-chat, yet applied successfully for the post of ambassador to the United States, the country he had selected as the best military and political ally for Israel. He made no secret of his personal aversion to the late Yassir Arafat, but, as Prime Minister, developed a working relationship with him during the Oslo years. He disliked any display of emotion, yet in his acceptance speech for the Nobel Prize on 10 December 1994 he spoke movingly of the many dead the conflict had taken, 'standing here today, I wish to salute and . . . I wish to pay tribute to each and every one of them, for this important prize is theirs, and theirs alone'. He was not a religious Jew, having been raised in the secular spirit of Jewish nationalism, but would not hear of sharing Jerusalem, the Jewish holy city, with his Palestinian 'partner' who laid equal claim to it. He was the first Israeli Prime Minister to openly advocate that only territorial concessions would lead to the security of the land of Israel. However, his rhetoric was often not only not supported by his policies but in fact contradicted by them. He was dubbed 'Mr. Security' by his countrymen, yet he died because no one heeded the warnings that his very own security could be under threat. He was murdered for what he ultimately failed to deliver. In a recent poll Yitzhak Rabin was named the most impressive Israeli figure and the top Israeli hero. It seems that only in death did he become the symbol of what could have been possible: a just peace between Israel and the Palestinians.

Rosa Cohen and Nehemiah Rabin: From Jewish Misery to the Zionist Dream

Yitzhak Rabin was born on 1 March 1922 in Jerusalem, Palestine. His parents Nehemiah Rabin and Rosa Cohen decided to name their firstborn after Rosa's father who had recently died. Nehemiah and Rosa were recent immigrants from Russia, both having fled the discrimination of the Tsarist regime and the persecution of its revolutionary successor.

The end of the 19th and the beginning of the 20th century were particularly difficult years for Russia's five million Jews. Waves of riots and pogroms tore through Jewish communities, leaving many dead and the survivors' lives in ruins. The Pale of Settlement, which was established by Tsarina Catherine II in 1791 and included present-day Latvia, Lithuania, Ukraine and Belorussia, limited the territory where 90 per cent of Russia's Jews were allowed to live and they were banned from taking out mortgages and loans. Other discriminatory laws restricted Jews attending universities and forced them into the Russian army. The Tsarist regime, authoritarian in character and oppressive in nature, despised its Jewish subjects and tacitly approved and even encouraged popular pogroms which were nurtured by religious anti-Semitism.

Nehemiah Robichov, or Rubitzov, was born in 1886, a period of relative calm after yet another wave of anti-Jewish violence. He was the son of a poor working-class family from Sidrovitch, near Kiev. When he was ten, following the early death of his father, he was forced to work at a local flour mill to help his mother make ends meet. A few years later he left his family, moving closer to Kiev, and continued working in the mill. During those years the young Nehemiah had his first encounter with socialism, an ideology that held great appeal for the Jews as its ideals and universal aspirations seemed to offer an escape from their pariah status and promised an end to discrimination. Even though he was far from being politically active, his tentative contacts were enough to arouse the suspicion of the local authorities, who wanted to detain him. Sensing his imminent arrest and fearing yet another series of pogroms, Nehemiah decided to flee the country. He was not alone in his decision: nearly half a million Jews had already done so. He arrived in New York in 1904 lonely, destitute and unable to speak the language. But he did not stay there long; after a brief period in St Louis, he eventually moved on to Chicago where he would spend the rest of his time in America. It was here that he became part of a group of young Jewish intellectuals who were not only socialists but also avid Zionists. Nehemiah had already heard about Zionism back in Russia but had 'shrugged [it] off . . . as an insignificant fringe movement'.[1]

Zionism, the movement of secular Jewish nationalism, emerged in the second half of the 19th century as a direct result of the general rise of secular nationalism and the failure of the promise of Jewish emancipation – that all men could assimilate as individuals into their respective societies – in Western Europe and the latent anti-Semitism in Eastern Europe. While Jews in the West at first made progress towards legal and social equality, their brethren in Eastern Europe, after a brief period of calm, went through a difficult period of exclusion, persecution and open hostility. In the late 19th century several groups sprang up which proposed not only the emancipation of the Jews but their treatment not just as a religious group but as a nation like other nations. Gradually the idea evolved that the Jewish nation should have a home, its own territory where the Jews could live. And eventually the idea of Palestine, the home of the ancient Hebrews and the never-forgotten place of their origin, the 'promised land', became the focus of Jewish dreams and aspirations and at the end of the 19th century the first Jews settled in Palestine, then under Ottoman jurisdiction. Zionism, the mere idea of self-help by Jews for Jews, was met with fierce opposition by the Orthodox Jewish establishment. Religious Jews were vehemently opposed to the Zionists' activist approach which clashed with their belief that their salvation depended entirely on God's intervention. But faced with continuing violent anti-Semitism in the East and the new anti-Semitism in the West, where the old ghetto walls were quickly replaced by less visible but no less impenetrable ones, Zionism gained momentum. Jewish nationalism finally gained international recognition after one man successfully managed to place the Jews' quest for a homeland on the international agenda: the Viennese journalist Theodor Herzl. Herzl was born in Budapest in 1860 but settled in Vienna at the age of 18. He studied law and became an attorney, but soon afterwards his interest turned to literature and the theatre. In time he moved to France where he became a correspondent for the Viennese newspaper *Neue Freie Presse*. It was in Paris that Herzl, until that time an ardent advocate of Jewish assimilation into the societies of the countries where they were living, witnessed a shocking example of anti-Semitism which completely changed his belief that Jewish emancipation in Western Europe constituted an irreversible, positive trend. The catalyst for his decision to commit himself to the solution of the Jewish problem, as he would call it, was the infamous Dreyfus affair. Alfred Dreyfus was a Jewish-French army officer who was falsely accused of treason and sentenced to life imprisonment on Devil's Island. His trial and the subsequent scandal brought out unknown depths of violent anti-Semitism in France. Herzl, who reported on the trial, responded to these shocking events by writing his famous book *Der Judenstaat* which ultimately established him as the leader of world Zionism. Yet, he did not only propagate the Jewish state in his writings, he also relentlessly rallied political support for the solution of the pressing 'Jewish question' and introduced it to European statesmen and wealthy Western Jews, whose financial support he needed. In 1897 Herzl convened a congress in Basel where he formed the World Zionist Organisation. He helped to set up such crucial bodies as the Jewish National Fund and the World Zionist Bank, which were instrumental in preparing the ground for the foundation of a Jewish state, although he never insisted that Palestine was the only place where Jews might settle. But Zionism did not just have political aims: it also aimed to transform the Jews themselves from a predominantly religious community into a nation with their own language, territory and economy. It strove in essence for a normalisation of the Jews and rejected perceived Jewish narrow-mindedness and its preoccupation with religious studies and most of all their quiet acceptance and endurance of their fate. Many Russian Jews, who were predominant in the shaping of the Zionist movement and later the Israeli state, had witnessed the socialist revolutions of 1905 and 1917. Thus they combined Zionism with socialist ideals and tried to implement them in Palestine by creating an egalitarian Jewish society based on socialist principles which would eventually transform the Jews and turn the people of the Book, the Bible, into a physically strong, worldly and essentially modern people.

The more time Nehemiah spent with these young men, who were constantly engaged in heated political debates and discussions, the more he became fascinated by Zionism. It was mostly due to their influence that, after the outbreak of the First World War, he decided to join the newly-established Jewish Legion. The Legion was formed in 1914 by Zionist leaders, among them Ze'ev Jabotinsky and David Ben Gurion, as a military formation of Jewish volunteers to aid the British during the First World War. It included British volunteers, and a large number of Russian Jews. Nehemiah too wanted to go to Palestine and help the Allies fight the German Empire and to further the establishment of a Jewish national home. Initially an officious recruiter disqualified him because of an alleged problem with his feet, but Nehemiah did not give up and simply tried his luck at another recruiting office under a slightly altered name and as Nehemiah Rabin he was happily accepted into the ranks of the Jewish Legion. He left the United States, a place he had grown very fond of, for Palestine in 1917.

It was that same year that the British Foreign Secretary Lord Balfour declared that 'His Majesty's Government view with favour the establishment in Palestine of a national home for the Jewish people'.[2] The Balfour Declaration, as it became known, was a major breakthrough for Zionist leaders, especially Chaim Weizmann who later became Israel's first President and had lobbied persistently for British support. Britain had perceived Palestine, which was then still part of the Ottoman Empire, as a possible buffer zone between French-controlled Syria and Lebanon and British-held Egypt. The two colonial powers had competing territorial interests in the region, which they had tried to settle in the Anglo-French Agreement of 1915 which established their two spheres of influence.

Rosa arrived two years later. Unlike her future husband, she was born into a wealthy merchant family in the little Russian town of Mohilov in 1890. Her father, Rabbi Yitzhak Cohen, was a devoutly religious man and had little or no appreciation for worldly ideas like socialism and Zionism; according to him they were approaching heresy. After his wife's death he moved his family to Homel to be closer to his brother, Mordechai Ben Hillel Hacohen, and his family. Mordechai, on the other hand, was convinced that the fate of the Jews, considering their precarious situation, could not be left entirely in the hands of God and was a staunch Zionist. As a response to the pogroms of the 1870s and 1890s, during which hundred of Jews were brutally murdered, he packed his belongings, took his family and, only a year after his brother had arrived in Homel, moved to Palestine. Despite the new pogroms and his brother's radical reaction to them, Rabbi Cohen was undeterred and continued to raise his children strictly according to Jewish religious custom. Once Rosa started to attend the local Christian Gymnasium, her father explicitly forbid her to attend any classes on Saturday, the Jewish Shabbat and day of rest. But Rosa was a stubborn and determined child and she soon managed to get her own way: she simply told her father that she would spend the night and day with a friend and thus was able to attend the classes against her father's unequivocal orders. Rosa was proud to be Jewish and felt compassion for their fate. But she was never an outright Zionist and the idea of leaving her native country never entered her mind. Not even the pogrom of 1905, when she served as a nurse, and which triggered another mass wave of Jewish emigration, could change her mind; she wanted to stay in Russia and be part of the revolutionary movement. In 1917 she went to Petrograd and enrolled in the Polytechnic Institute for Women. But the long-awaited Bolshevik Revolution did not bring the changes Rosa had hoped for. On the contrary, the overall situation, especially for the Jews, went progressively from bad to worse. The new Revolutionaries did not differ much in their attitude towards Jews from the old regime and even treated Zionism as yet another reason to persecute Jews. In the end the situation got out of hand and Rosa, who by then had quit her studies to work as a bookkeeper in a factory and shared her wages with the poorest, reluctantly decided to leave the country that simply did not want her. Persecuted by the new Bolshevik police and always in danger of being arrested, she joined the Red Cross and boarded a train to the port city of Odessa. Her plan was to join some friends in Sweden, but since the only ship sailing any time soon was the *Russland* whose destination was Palestine, she decided to board it. At the age of 28 she reached the shores of Palestine, a place which she was convinced would only be her new home temporarily.

Rosa and Nehemiah met in April 1920. They were both in Jerusalem at a time when tensions between Jews and Palestinians had intensified once again and exploded in violent riots. Britain, which had been awarded the Mandate for Palestine by the League of Nations that same year, had difficulty coping with the conflicting aims of its mandate. On the one hand Britain was to facilitate the creation of a Jewish national home while at the same time it was supposed to protect the rights of the existing local population. This dual, inconsistent commitment resulted in escalating rivalry between Jews and Palestinian Arabs that an increasingly strained Britain was unable to manage.

Their first meeting, which took place in the middle of anti-Jewish riots in Jerusalem, resulted in a heated argument. Nehemiah, who was part of a newly-formed Jewish defence committee, called out angrily to the passing Rosa, who was serving as a nurse, demanding to know what she was doing in such a dangerous place. They ended up screaming at each other in Yiddish and had to be separated by British soldiers. Only after establishing that they were actually fighting for the same side, were they able to calm down and speak to each other in a more civilised manner: it was the awkward beginning of the romance of Nehemiah Rabin and Rosa Cohen. Their son would later laconically remark that 'one thing led to another, and he married my mother in 1921'.[3]

Rosa, who decided to keep her maiden name, became pregnant almost immediately afterwards. By and large she welcomed her condition but she was determined it would not stop her from fulfilling the many duties she had taken upon herself; she continued working until she was well into her ninth month. By then she was convinced that Palestine, this climatic and political hotbed, was her home. Her new mission was the realisation of Zionism. After a brief stint in a Kibbutz, a small agricultural community which embodied the ideals of secular

Zionism as well as those of socialism by emphasising the necessity of self-reliance, social cohesion and communal living, on the shores of Sea of Galilee and a short visit to her uncle Mordechai who had settled in Jerusalem, she found a job in Haifa with a timber firm owned by relatives. In addition she also helped to establish a medical co-operative for workers, loudly demanded that the 'railway system, postal service, and police force [should] hire Jews'[4] instead of cheaper Palestinian Arab workers (which ran counter to the socialists' belief in promoting a genuine labour movement but was deemed necessary to facilitate the Jewish national cause), and she was instrumental in organising a Jewish military defence force, the Hagana.

It was decided that Rosa should give birth in Jerusalem where her family lived. But shortly after Yitzhak was born she was eager to return to Haifa and to get on with her work; giving birth and the resulting convalescence were a shameful waste of time. With difficulty she was persuaded by her husband and uncle to stay in Jerusalem a little bit longer to rest, but after only four weeks she was back in Haifa and a very early age the baby Yitzhak had to get used to the fact that his mother was not his alone but felt responsible for everyone.

A Son of Working Parents:
Early Years and School Days

In 1923 Nehemiah, a quiet and easygoing man, was offered a job at the Palestine Electric Corporation in Tel Aviv and the family decided to move. The bubbly and energetic Rosa had, in the meantime, become the Hagana's first commander, notwithstanding the fact that she was a woman, lacked any military experience and possessed only a rudimentary command of Hebrew. Yitzhak was cared for by friends. Two years later, while she was working for the Soleh Boneh building contractors as an accountant, Rosa somehow managed to fit in another baby: Yitzhak's sister Rachel was born in 1925. The expansion of the family did not cause Rosa to slow down. With parents who took on a range of voluntary work in addition to their day jobs, there was little time spent as a family. Yitzhak would later describe the atmosphere at home as 'ours was a workers' home' where he and his sister were trained from an early age to assume 'responsibilities at home: making beds, washing dishes, and sweeping floors'.[5] Rosa was barely at home and it fell to Nehemiah, who worked more regular hours, to provide the family with a regular framework. But apart from the breakfasts and dinners he prepared for them, the children continued to be mainly looked after by friends and neighbours. Once Yitzhak was a little bit older he had to look after his sister and dutifully took her wherever he went. Rachel would later recall that only after she became a mother herself did she realise how well her brother had given her the kind of emotional security her absent parents could never provide.[6] But it was an entirely different story for Yitzhak. Many years later, in a series of radio interviews called 'The House of my Father', broadcast shortly after the June 1967 war, he offered a rare insight into his emotions and admitted the profound loneliness he experienced as a child.

In 1928, at the age of six, he was enrolled at the Beit Hinuch, a school for workers' children founded by his mother who was eager to provide educational institutions which had little in common with traditional bourgeois ones. The school was housed in a plain wooden barrack, close to a park. The children were not only asked to grow vegetables in an allotted plot but also to prepare them for their lunch. It was essentially an elite institution for future leaders where only few applicants were accepted and most of them were children of prominent labour leaders. The children were educated in a system that placed 'education before instruction, inculcating values before imparting book learning'. His first days at school were not happy ones: 'Mother had no time to ease me through the first days of school' and 'I found myself standing there confused and on the brink of tears'.[7] He eventually adapted to his new surroundings, enjoying the classes while keeping mostly to himself. He was an easy prey for other children's mockery: he was a timid boy whose natural inhibition made it difficult for him to relate to his classmates who liked to mock him for 'his reddish hair and tendency to blush'[8] and who took his shyness for calculated aloofness.

Much more worrying than his classmates' teasing was his mother's failing health. Rosa had suffered for years from a weak heart and Yitzhak grew up in the shadow of his mother's illness. When Rosa's health deteriorated further the young boy felt increasingly terrified that he 'would return' one day from school 'and find her dead'.[9] Since he had no close friends and 'did not show my feelings or share them with others'[10] his way of releasing tension and stress, both at home and at school, was a solitary one: he began his life-long habit of heavy smoking.

In 1935 he graduated and went to a regional intermediary school in Kibbutz Givat Hashlosha near Tel Aviv. Again it was a school his busy mother had founded. It was an institution that closely followed Zionist ideals and prepared city children, just like her son, for a rural life in a Kibbutz, the perceived ideal way of life at the time. After two years at Givat Hashlosha, Yitzhak took an entry exam to the prestigious Kadoorie Agricultural School. When he passed the exam only conditionally and had to sit another exam, he was shocked and his 'pride wounded'.[11] Following extensive tutoring by a neighbour, he passed the second time with flying colours.

The British-sponsored Kadoorie was completely different from his other schools; run like a British boarding school, it did not offer any of the freedom he had enjoyed so far but was instead run on firm discipline and in an 'autocratic manner' under which Yitzhak surprisingly flourished. He became an excellent student, was not too bothered by the 'tyranny and tricks' of older students who, following old boarding school tradition, enjoyed giving the newcomers a hard time, and even slowly started to gain his fellow students' respect.[12] But just as he was settling in, his mother became gravely ill. In addition to her heart problems, Rosa had also developed cancer. Yitzhak returned immediately to Tel Aviv wanting 'to believe that she knew that I was on my way and had called up her last ounce of strength to hold on'.[13] He found his mother barely conscious. Rosa, aged 47, died shortly afterwards. Her funeral was attended by thousands of people, family, friends, countless labour officials as well as all those she had helped with such vigour throughout the few years she had lived in Palestine. Despite her physical absence during most of her children's lives her death was a most traumatic experience. Rachel hardly remembered her mother, but Yitzhak did and her life as well as her untimely death would influence his whole life; particularly the sense that he had to live up to the high standards she had set by her relentless work, sense of duty and responsibility. After the traditional seven days of mourning, Yitzhak returned to Kadoorie with the feeling that he 'had crossed over the threshold of manhood'[14] and set about dedicating himself exclusively to his studies. Political developments, however, would soon steer him, like most youngsters of his generation, away from his chosen path.

A Soldier by Chance

By the late 1930s the once tiny Jewish community, the Yishuv, had grown into a strong society. United and single-minded, the Zionist leadership had been able to win from the British permission to set up various bodies to organise Jewish affairs, stipulate immigration and allow for the acquisition of more and more land. In particular the Yishuv's relative independence from the Mandate power in managing its own cultural, political and economic affairs created a growing gap between the Jews and Palestinians Arabs.

Already well before the Mandate period the native Palestinian Arabs resented Zionist intrusion into their land. Even though Palestinian Arab nationalism, like elsewhere in the Arab world, developed rather late and was often focussed on union with another Arab country – in Palestine's case preferably Syria – it was a strong sentiment which was only accentuated by the increasing influx of Zionist settlers who made no secret of the fact that they wanted the land for their future state. Shortly after the First World War Palestinian Arab intellectuals drew up a petition which denounced the Balfour Declaration. It stated that while the Palestinians 'sympathised profoundly with the persecuted Jews and their misfortunes in other countries . . . there is a wide difference between this sympathy and the acceptance of such a [Jewish] nation . . . ruling over us and disposing of our affairs'.[15] And they demanded that Palestine should not only remain an Arab country but also have the same right to self-determination as had been granted to Egypt, Transjordan and Iraq. Already in the early years of the 20th century Arabs and Jews had engaged in violent clashes and riots as a result of the Arabs' 'disappointment of their political and national aspirations and fear for their economic future',[16] fears and frustration that only grew over the years and let to even more violent riots in the mid-1920s as Jewish efforts to turn the promised 'national home' into a Jewish state increased. The British had difficulties from the beginning in containing these clashes, which was due partly to the impossible provisions of its Mandate and partly to Britain's ambiguous policies and objectives. British officials in Palestine were generally sympathetic to Palestinian Arabs and often at odds with their political counterparts in London, many of whom thought that Zionism was the main reason for their presence and the justification for their occupation. Only during the run-up to the Second World War did London react to growing Arab opposition and repudiate the Balfour Declaration by restricting immigration and halting land sales. The greatest worries to the Palestinians were the ever-increasing numbers of Jewish immigrants and the rise of land sales. The rise in Palestinian peasants' sale of land to Jews was chiefly a result of the economic situation of Palestine under the British Mandate which made it open for exploitation 'in classic colonial fashion'. While the Jews enjoyed an economic boom in the 1930s thanks to the influx of new immigrants and their capital, Arab peasants and small landowners suffered a steady decline in their economic situation which created a vicious circle: to ease their plight they sold more land which in turn fuelled the conflict over land.[17] In 1936 the Mufti of Jerusalem, Haj Amin el-Husseini, one of the most prominent Palestinian Arab leaders, organised a general strike that led to a broad-based and popular Arab revolt against Jewish immigration and land purchases, and advocated the replacement of the Mandate with a representative Palestinian Arab government. The revolt lasted altogether for three years and eventually led to a British-led inquiry into the causes of the uprising. The Peel Commission, which issued its final report in 1937, proposed partition of the land. It suggested that a Jewish state should comprise one-third of Palestine and an Arab state in the rest of the territory that would merge with Transjordan. The Palestinians rejected the idea since it denied them statehood, while the Zionists approved of the idea of a state but merely saw it as a starting point to eventually negotiate more territory.

A year after the rebellion broke out it reached the north of Palestine. In anticipation of Arab attacks the students of Kadoorie received their first military training. Their instructor was Yigal Allon, a sergeant in the Hagana, nicknamed the 'King of Galilee', who was widely admired by the pupils as epitomising the image of the new Jewish fighter. Three weeks before the end of Yitzhak's first year, the British decided to close the school as a security precaution. Allon had taken a liking to Yitzhak and asked him to join a military camp at Kibbutz Ginossar. He spent six months there, working in the fields and on guard duty, and then moved for an additional six months of military training to Kvutzat Ha'Sharon. One month after the outbreak of the Second World War, the school

17

reopened and Yitzhak resumed his studies. He graduated, again with flying colours, in August 1940.

His military service was meant to be only temporary; Yitzhak had no intention of becoming a soldier but still dreamt of working in a kibbutz. His principal, impressed by his academic achievements, had arranged a scholarship for him to the University of Berkeley in California to study hydraulic engineering. It was a move his father also strongly supported and which suited Yitzhak who thought that it was a subject worthy of study considering the importance of water for the future realisation of his Zionist dreams. However, he was not to pursue his studies immediately.

Due to German advances in North Africa, the British sought support from the Yishuv and approved of the establishment of a separate Jewish fighting force under the umbrella of the Hagana, the Palmach. Initially it was to be a 'striking force' of full-time volunteers to meet the danger of an Axis invasion but once the Second World War was over it became the principal force of the Hagana in the struggle against Britain. Yitzhak had not been overly enthusiastic about the idea of the Jews helping the hated Mandate power, after it imposed restrictions on Jewish immigration in 1939 after Germany's invasion of Czechoslovakia. The White Paper was intended to win Arab support in the fight against Nazi Germany and to that end Britain in fact reversed its policy by stating that 'it is not part of British policy that Palestine should become a Jewish state' and consequently heavily restricted Jewish immigration and land purchase. The paper was met by Arab doubts about its seriousness and Jewish outrage since it endangered the whole Zionist endeavour. When the local Hagana commander asked him to volunteer, Yitzhak, with little hesitation, decided to postpone his studies for the time being and agreed.

First the Axis, then the British:
1940–1947

While the 30,000 Jews from the Yishuv who had joined the British regular forces were rigged out in smart uniforms, polished boots and berets, the 'Palmachniks', as the fighters of the Palmach became known, wore rather shabby clothes and committed themselves to the rather thankless task of working outside the limelight. In 1941 the Palmach commandos eventually went into action during the British attack on Lebanon and Syria which were under the control of Vichy France. They had been divided into two forces, one led by Yigal Allon, the other by Moshe Dayan. One of Yitzhak's first missions for the Palmach was to cross the Lebanese border secretly in advance of Australian forces to cut the telephone lines and prevent 'the Vichy French from rushing reinforcement to the area'. It was 'not exactly battlefield high drama'[18] but an important mission nevertheless. Yitzhak's group was ordered to infiltrate Lebanon between the cities of Zur and Sidon along the coast.[19] The group completed the task successfully, despite their lack of equipment and limited training.

The successful raid boosted Yitzhak's reputation; especially during the lectures he gave afterwards where he was able to show his clear analytical mind and methodical thinking. In 1942, when the Allies feared that the Germans might overrun Palestine, the British turned once more to the Palmach for further sabotage and demolitions. Yitzhak was sent to a special training camp near Kibbutz Mishmar Ha' Emek where he and his comrades received training in 'topography, tracking and map-reading'.[20] By early 1943, however, after the victory at El Alamein and the subsequent German retreat, the British decided that the usefulness of the Palmach had run its course. Furthermore, they quite correctly feared that the increased military experience and success of the Jewish armed forces might pose a serious threat to their rule. Therefore they ordered the dispersal of the training camp and the uneasy relationship between the Mandate power and the Yishuv entered a new phase. The British wanted to dampen the hopes of the Yishuv that a Jewish state was in the making. They also intended to curb their military strength. It did not go unnoticed that the Jews had not only been given weapons by the British but had also been acquiring them by clandestine raids on British arms depots. But it was too late: by 1943 the Palmach began its first independent military actions.

Yitzhak had been promoted to Platoon Commander. He was stationed in the Kibbutz Kfar Giladi near the Lebanese border and trained young men in military tactics when he and his pupils were not working the fields. It was at this time that an incident occurred which nearly cost him his military career almost before it had begun. His platoon had to present a fire display before senior officers of the Hagana in a Kibbutz near Haifa. When one mortar shell failed to fire Rabin decided to take it: after all, his platoon had mortars but no shells, a 'serious defect' he 'felt obliged to correct'. But it was an illegal and dangerous 'correction', since the Hagana had issued strict orders that no one was allowed to carry weapons openly for fear of being detected by British. A week later and 'thoroughly satisfied' that he had been able to bring the mortar shell home undetected, his company commander approached him. He informed Yitzhak that a shell was missing and wanted to know whether he knew anything about its whereabouts. Yitzhak, 'like the apocryphal George Washington faced with the evidence of his cherry-tree crime . . . could not tell a lie', admitted the offence. As a result he was notified a few days later that he would be court-martialled. The next few days he spent 'like in a trance', worried and sleeping very little. In the end he got off lightly: no promotion for a year. In his memoirs, however, he wrote proudly that in 1947, when he was the Palmach's Chief of Operations and an inventory of weapons were made, '"my" shell was the only one the Palmach possessed'.[21]

By the end of the Second World War, the question of Palestine's future became more and more pressing and it was a combination of internal and external factors that led to the eventual withdrawal of Britain and to the establishment of the State of Israel. The horrors of the Holocaust, which became known in the early 1940s, caused many American Jews, who had previously only expressed quiet support of the establishment of a Jewish state, to make themselves heard more forcefully. In 1942 they organised a conference and concluded their meeting with the recommendation of the Biltmore Program. It openly backed Jewish immigration and the establishment of a Jewish state in Palestine and called for the Jews to intensively campaign for those aims among US voters and politicians.[22] The incoming American president Harry Truman publicly approved of the program and was able, thanks to America's growing economic and military power, to exert political pressure to that end.

The official Jewish leadership, led by David Ben Gurion, had only agreed to work with the British for tactical reasons. The Yishuv still believed that a strong power like Britain would be instrumental in attaining a state and the predominant need in the early 1940s was a British victory over Germany. Once the war had ended, however, the fight for a Jewish state would begin in earnest and the Jews knew that they would need not only to overcome Palestinian but also British resistance. To that end the Yishuv had effectively used the war years to arm and prepare itself for an all-out military confrontation. It was aided (and sometimes hindered) by emerging Jewish terrorist groups, which increasingly stepped up their attacks on British infrastructure and personnel. The principal group was a faction of the military arm of the Revisionists, a territorial and political maximalist party which was founded in 1925 and which only five years later withdrew from the Zionist movement over serious disagreements as to how and where exactly to achieve a Jewish state. In 1931 it established the Irgun, an independent right-wing militia led by Menachem Begin that employed guerrilla tactics to drive out the British. In 1940 Lehi, also called the Stern Gang, seceded from the Irgun and launched terrorist attacks against the Mandate Power and later the Palestinians, and at times openly challenged the Zionist leadership and their strategy. Particularly noteworthy was the bombing of the King David Hotel, which the British used as their headquarters, by the Irgun in April 1946 when 91 people were killed. The Palestinians, who after the failed revolt of 1936 and the subsequent war years found themselves leaderless and in disarray, sensed Britain's growing weariness and were alarmed by the increasing efforts of the Jews to prepare themselves for an armed conflict to establish their state. As a result they too increased their military resistance, and started to openly oppose British rule. They targeted British officials and armed bands roamed Palestine, attacking each other and Jews alike.

By 1947 the situation was becoming more and more untenable and Britain turned to the United Nations to make recommendations on the status and future of Palestine. The UN General Assembly eventually proposed the partition of Palestine and narrowly endorsed the plan as Resolution 181 on 29 November. The Arab Higher Committee, founded in 1944, rejected the plan, favouring a single state in Palestine, and thus strongly opposed the establishment of separate Jewish and Palestinian states. The Jews, represented by the leaders of the Yishuv, accepted it after some initial hesitation, and so, while Britain was preparing to pull its troops out, no longer willing to commit men and resources to a lost cause, a civil war broke out between the Jews and the Palestinians.

The Inter-War Years: 1945–1947

During the two years between the end of the Second World War and the beginning of what became Israel's War of Independence, Rabin continued to work on the Kibbutz and to receive and give further military training. Despite his earlier block on promotion, he first became an instructor of the Palmach's First Battalion and later on the commander of the national section-leaders' course. When in October 1945 the Yishuv started their campaign against the British in earnest, the First Battalion was ordered to break into a detention camp for refugees near Atlit on the Mediterranean coast south of Haifa. The aim was to free about 200 immigrants, all survivors of the Holocaust, whom the British intended to deport. Yitzhak, who was deputy commander of the operation, exploited the fact that the British allowed welfare workers and teachers to enter the camp, and infiltrated some of his men disguised as teachers. It was a moonless night when Rabin and his comrades set out on their mission. To their great surprise they met little resistance: the

Arab guards' weapons would not fire and the British soldiers were fast asleep. What proved to be much more difficult was convincing the refugees to part with their small bundles of luggage which were often their last remaining possessions, and to make men, women and children leave the camp quickly and quietly. The plan was to shepherd the refugees to trucks which would bring them to Kibbutz Bet Oren while some men would stay behind to prevent the British from halting the rescue operation. But soon things went wrong: realising that their suitcases and bundles were in fact less important than their lives, the refugees dropped them one by one, leaving a trail for the British to follow. Rabin and Uri Sarig, the Battalion's First Commander, hastily decided to change their plan and split the refugees in two groups. Sarig would guide the stronger ones to the waiting trucks while Rabin would accompany the weaker ones on foot to nearby Kibbutz Yagur, hoping that reinforcements would soon arrive. While Sarig and the first group of refugees reached the Kibbutz shortly before dawn, Rabin – carrying a frightened youngster on his shoulders who occasionally peed on his back – made only gradual progress. When he spotted British troops near the Kibbutz he decided to hide in the woods and wait. But two of his men found a gap in the British cordon and he attempted to break through. In the end he managed to bring all the refugees into the Kibbutz and ordered them to quickly disperse. But the British soldiers had followed them and stood at the gates of the Kibbutz, desperately trying to find a way to break in and to recapture the refugees and the men responsible for their escape. Once they realised that this could only be done at the cost of causing heavy casualties, they withdrew. Rabin was very pleased with his success and finally 'could change his wet clothes'.[23]

Not only his military career prospered; his private life had also taken a pleasant turn. In the summer of 1943 he had met a young girl who, once she had set eyes on the handsome yet shy soldier, decided that he was to be hers. Leah Schlossberg was born on 8 April 1928 in Königsberg in East Prussia into a wealthy, upper-middle-class industrialist family. She had arrived in Palestine with her mother, her older sister Aviva and their nursemaid Trüdel in the summer of 1933 to join her father, Fima Schlossberg, who had left Germany immediately after Adolf Hitler had been appointed Chancellor on 31 January 1933 to prepare for his family's arrival. Despite the adverse political developments in Germany, Leah's parents never gave up their German culture and their daughters received and 'absorbed an extensive cultural foundation'.[24] Leah differed from Yitzhak not only socially and culturally; their personalities were also radically different: she was a bois-terous, open and talkative person who easily made friends and sometimes, due to her outspokenness, enemies. She loved to entertain people and later would widely use her talents as a hostess to advance her husband's career. Yitzhak, on the other hand, would only on rare occasions overcome his withdrawn nature, gruff manner and unease in social settings. Leah's first impression of Yitzhak during their first chance encounter in an ice-cream parlour in Tel Aviv was that of the ancient 'King David'. Like most girls of her age she was enthralled by the mystery that surrounded the fighters of the Palmach, 'the young underground guardians whose dreams and energy would create and defend a Jewish state'.[25] Yitzhak, on the other hand and with his typical understatement would recall the beginning of their 'wartime romance' as 'a glance, a word, a stirring, and then a further meeting'. At the beginning it was

27

difficult for them to meet; Yitzhak could rarely get leave and Leah still lived with her parents in Tel Aviv. But when she joined the Palmach in 1945 and started to serve in his battalion, 'one of the rare occasions she was under my command' as he would dryly remark in his memoirs, he was able to meet her more often between missions.[26]

After the successful rescue mission at Atlit, Yitzhak was assigned the task of attacking a British police station. He got into the station disguised as an electrician equipped with screwdrivers and other tools to scout out the station's layout in preparation for the attack. But on his way back to the Palmach's headquarters on his motorcycle, while 'cheerfully roaring along' a truck made a sudden sharp turn in front of him which left him no time to avoid a collision. When he later woke up in Rothschild Hospital in Haifa, a comrade, trying somewhat clumsily to cheer him up, dutifully reported that they had found his left ankle which was just by his knee. His serious injury forced a lengthy convalescence at his father's home in Tel Aviv, on crutches and unable to take part in further operations and cursing his fate.[27] But being out of action did not save him from being tracked down by the British. The Mandate power, fed up with the increasing attacks from the Jewish right and left, began its most comprehensive effort to put an end to the increasing disorder. On 26 June 1946, a day the Jews would from then on call 'Black Saturday', Yitzhak, together with his father and thousands of other Jewish fighters, were arrested. Still hobbling on crutches he was brought first to a detention camp in Latrun and later to Rafah, in the Gaza Strip. Nearly the entire leadership of the Yishuv, save Ben Gurion, who was at that time in the United States, were caught. During his enforced stay he received, courtesy of the

British, medical treatment for his broken leg and regular physiotherapy, which gradually improved his condition. When his cast was removed he was shocked and depressed to find his leg 'misshapen and lifeless' and was convinced he would spent the rest of his life as a 'semicripple'.[28] He spend his days miserably in the noisy and overcrowded camp writing letters to his family and Leah – his father had been released after three weeks – and seriously thinking about his future. Since a military career seemed now to be out of the question, he decided to take up the offer from Berkeley and pursue his studies.

Upon his release in November, still hobbling along with a cane, he reported back to Yigal Allon and told him of his decision. Allon neither wanted to hear about Rabin's perceived state of health nor his plans to abandon the military for academia, and, as Rabin recalled, countered his suggestion by saying 'The world war has ended but our war is only just beginning'.[29] Yitzhak once more postponed his studies and, only a week later, took command of the Palmach's Second Battalion.

The War of 1948

The six months between the United Nations vote in favour of the partition of Palestine and Israel's declaration of independence saw a flurry of activity on all sides. While the international community was still considering the implications of their vote, the Palestinians and Arab leaders, hampered by rivalries and suspicion of each others' motives, tried to organise not only diplomatic but also military resistance to partition. The Jews, under the undisputed leadership of Ben Gurion, were mainly concerned about whether they would be able to acquire in the coming conflict all the territory that was allotted to them according to the partition plan.[30] The plan envisioned the establishment of both a Jewish and a Palestinian state and a zone that would fall under international control, namely Jerusalem and Bethlehem. According to the plan 14,000 square kilometres, with a population of 558,000 Jews and 405,000 Arabs, was to become the Jewish state, and 11,500 square kilometres, with a population of 804,000 Arabs and a clear Jewish minority of 10,000 would become an Arab state.

31

The plan further envisioned an economic union between the two states, jointly-controlled railways, a single currency and shared control over the ports of Haifa and Jaffa.

The subsequent war between the Jews and their Palestinian and Arab opponents went through several stages. Initially it mainly featured Arab guerrilla attacks on Jewish settlements on whose defence the Hagana concentrated.[31] But by March 1948, after the Hagana had suffered several defeats at the hands of Palestinian irregulars, the Jews decided on an offensive strategy that was to be 'accompanied by economic subversion and psychological warfare'. This strategy became known as Plan D and its aim was not only to secure the areas allocated to the Jewish State according to the UN partition plan but also to link Jewish settlements outside of it with the main territory. This involved attacks on and possible capture of Arab villages and cities, thus setting in motion the disintegration of Palestinian society and resulting in the expulsion of Palestinian civilians, which was reinforced by the early departure of Palestinian leaders who preferred to watch events from a safe distance.[32] This plan was put into force after Ben Gurion declared the independent state of Israel on 14 May 1948. It was immediately attacked by the armies of Egypt, Syria, Lebanon, Transjordan and Iraq.

In the winter of 1947 Rabin, at the age of 25, had been promoted to lead the Second Battalion's strike force. It was actually a job for a more experienced soldier but Yigal Allon chose him. In April 1948 he was made commander of the Harel Brigade which was assigned to 'eliminating the Arab bases along the Tel Aviv–Jerusalem road'.[33] Keeping that road open was essential since the city and its inhabitants depended on the supply trucks that made their way up the narrow road leading to the city. The city of Jerusalem is holy to both sides:

for the Jews it is the eternal city where their ancient temple once stood and the remaining Western Wall which is central to their prayers. To Muslims Jerusalem is the third holiest city and the place from where their prophet is said to have ascended to heaven. The city had also always been the centre of Palestinian social and cultural life, while a Jewish presence, despite the prolonged exile, had never ceased to exist. Thus the battle for the road and later the city itself was a fierce one.

On one occasion Rabin was directly involved in the expulsion of Palestinians when Jewish forces went once more on the offensive during ten days of fighting between the first and second truce. In his memoirs he called it a 'troublesome problem' and he referred to the 'fate of the civilian population of Lod and Ramle'.[34] When Yigal Allon asked Ben Gurion what they were supposed to do with the Palestinian population, Ben Gurion reportedly 'waved his hand in a gesture that said: Drive them out!'[35] Rabin agreed with the necessity of Ben Gurion's order but recalled that the expulsion was psychologically very difficult. The official line for many years was that all the Palestinians either fled voluntarily or on the orders of their leaders. Only later would Israel concede that some had been driven out by force, thus undermining one of the founding myths of the young state by which it sought moral superiority. In addition to fighting for land and rearranging the population balance in Israel's favour, Rabin made use of the brief second truce to undergo some 'personal "reorganisation"':[36] he married Leah on 23 August 1948. Their wedding took place in Tel Aviv. Notwithstanding their four-year-long relationship he was still very inhibited about Leah and intentionally misinformed his friends and comrades about the timing of the wedding, telling them that it would start 30 minutes later than it was actually planned to. But the Rabbi was late and by the time he arrived all the guests were there too. Having finally survived the embarrassment and ceremony alike he proclaimed that 'this is absolutely the last time I am getting married'.[37] They did not have much time to get used to their marital state as Yitzhak was summoned to a meeting about military operations in the south. Their home for the next years was Leah's parents' house; a decision which was born not only out of their lack of funds but also out of the ailing health of her parents. When they finally had time to go on their honeymoon in the coastal town of Naharia, winter had already arrived and Yitzhak suffered from toothache.[38]

In January 1949 the war was finally brought to an end by an armistice agreement. The Arab armies, despite being the combined forces of five countries, had been seriously outnumbered from the beginning by the Israelis and had suffered from poor training, poor equipment and poor leadership. Regardless of their military and tactical superiority, however, the Israelis had won a costly victory: while territorial gains left Israel in charge of more land than the 1947 plan had allocated to it, the young state had lost 6,000 soldiers and civilians, about 1 per cent of its population[39] and had been on the brink of civil war when the Jewish right, led by Menachem Begin, had daringly defied Ben Gurion in the run-up to and during the war, but eventually Ben Gurion and the moderates had prevailed. The Arab states, notwithstanding their complete defeat, refused to accept its political consequences. Despite signing the ceasefire they refused to recognise the State of Israel since they saw it as the result of the illegal occupation of Palestine. In the years that followed most Arab states witnessed a period of internal upheaval and external rivalry triggered by their defeat and which would alter their countries and shape the course of the Arab–Israel conflict. For the Palestinians the 1948 War became known as 'al naqba', the 'catastrophe' or 'disaster'. It is estimated that between 300,000 and 700,000 Palestinian Arabs had either fled the Israeli Defence Force (IDF), the successor to the Hagana, or had been directly driven out. The most notorious incident was the massacre at Deir Yassin, where, despite an apparent non-aggression pact with the Hagana, 115 Palestinian men, women and children were killed by joint Irgun and Lehi forces who disposed of their bodies by throwing them down wells. The Hagana and Irgun publicised their deaths and disposal later with loudspeakers. The psychological impact was enormous and caused many Palestinians to flee their homes for fear of meeting the same fate.[40] They were either confined to refugee camps in various Arab countries or had fled either to the West Bank which fell under the jurisdiction of Jordan or to the Gaza Strip that was under Egyptian control. Israel, in turn, was busy overcoming the effects of war and trying to integrate thousands of new immigrants who flocked to the country from Arab states and war-torn Europe. The Jewish state tried its best to consolidate its presence and claim the land its soldiers had fought for. Israel considered the Palestinian refugees entirely an Arab responsibility since they had fled during a war the Arabs had imposed on Israel and in which Israel had to fight for nothing less than its survival, it claimed. Consequently the political establishment absolved itself from any responsibility and continued to deny the Palestinians not only national rights but also the right of constituting a separate nation. It was an attitude Israel would hold for decades and a point of view Yitzhak Rabin, like most members of what became know as the generation of 1948, fully subscribed to.

A Soldier by Choice: 1949–1968

The armistice talks between Egypt and Israel began on 13 January 1949 on the Greek island of Rhodes. Rabin, who had by then gained the nickname 'Analytical Brain', was made part of the Israeli delegation by order of Yigal Allon who wanted him to represent the Southern Front which had fought fierce battles with the Egyptians. Rabin was not enthusiastic to go: like his mentor, he felt that the job was not finished yet and that Israel, by entering premature armistice negotiations, would stop short of what was achievable and would in effect leave itself in a precarious security situation. Once he arrived at the Hotel of Roses where the delegations met, he found himself not only on a mission he did not like but also in the unfamiliar setting of polite diplomatic talk, formal pleasantries and battles that were fought with words rather than weapons. The circumstances demanded that he wore a smart uniform – not that smart since it had been bought at a second-hand shop in Tel Aviv – and a tie he had no idea how to knot and was 'terrified . . . might come undone'[41] at any moment, considerably adding to his unease. When the armistice agreement was finally about to be signed on 24 February, Rabin refused to do so. Above all he opposed the passage that would allow Egypt to get hold of Gaza, 'a slice of Palestine' as he complained to another delegate.[42] In a letter to Yigal Allon he grumbled that 'any concession now is too early. We have had a longer breathing space, and we can endure a war of nerves better that the Egyptians'.[43] Since his signature was not required for the agreement to come into effect he refused to put his name to it. He left Rhodes with the feeling that the accord opened the door to another round of fighting which he feared would come sooner rather than later.

Once he was back in Israel the question of his future came up again. The Palmach had been formally disbanded in November 1948 on the instructions of Ben Gurion. The official reason for this was to set up a unified army; but unofficially it was to break up an organisation whose members were associated with a political party who was a direct rival of Ben Gurion's party, Mapai, a forerunner of the Labour Party. When the former Palmachniks organised its third national conference in October 1949, a kind of farewell party, Ben Gurion went as far as banning serving officers from taking part in it. Rabin, still in uniform and one of the most senior officers of the former Palmach, was not deterred by the order and wanted to attend the meeting as a proof of his loyalty to his comrades; he regarded the matter as being one entirely of personal conscience rather than national politics. That same morning, however, he received a personal invitation from Ben Gurion to meet him at his home. It seemed Ben Gurion wanted to give Rabin an easy way out by offering him the plausible excuse that he could not attend the rally for he had been held up unexpectedly at the

Prime Minister's home. Rabin went but by early evening –
never good at small talk and anything but a natural diplomat
– he could no longer conceal his impatience and simply asked
Ben Gurion why he put former Palmach officers in such an
awkward position where they had to choose between the duty
'to maintain discipline' and the responsibility to 'comrades-in-
arms with whom we have come such a long way?'[44] Instead of
answering his question, Ben Gurion extended his invitation to
dinner. Rabin thanked him for his offer but excused himself,
saying that he was already engaged that night. He went
straight home, changed his clothes and attended the rally.
Days later, after he had been assigned to run a battalion-com-
mander's course, he was summoned once more to appear before
a court-martial. He knew that Ben Gurion might not forgive
his actions but his loyalty to his comrades was stronger than
his fear of the possible consequences. But now he feared the
worst and was hugely relieved that he was only reprimanded for
breach of discipline. Despite his immediate relief he sensed that
he might suffer repercussions for his defiance of Ben Gurion's
order in the years to come. He admired Ben Gurion's leadership,
but he had little respect for his political manoeuvring and was
never a party man which, given the fact that Ben Gurion's
Mapai was the dominant political force, was probably not the
most sensible idea.

More importantly he was not made to leave the armed
forces. True, he had once again entertained the idea of finally
studying hydraulic engineering, but now he actually wanted
to stay on in the army. It was a quite common desire among
his generation of young men who had fought in 1948; they
were attracted by the army's growing centrality and importance to the new state and were driven by the feeling that their

job was not yet completed and thus their services were still needed. But apart from this widespread sentiment, the experience of war, particularly the loss of many soldiers under his command, had left Rabin with a deep sense of 'moral responsibility, a kind of debt of honour'. And it was to the dead soldiers he felt compelled to swear an oath of allegiance and promised to ensure that 'the State of Israel would never again be unprepared to meet aggression'.[45] It was probably the first time that Rabin, who had become a soldier by chance and necessity rather than by rational choice, made a definite conscious decision concerning his future career.

But the disbanding of the Negev Brigade that same autumn left him with virtually no job. He learned with considerable interest about the organisation of a new course of instruction for officers, designed to impart unity and cohesion on the still quite makeshift Israeli army. Rabin's application to join it was accepted and he enjoyed teaching fellow officers and passing on his own experience as well as formulating new ideas and tactics, and most vitally developing a military doctrine that would be essentially Israeli and not reliant on the strategies the officers had learned while serving in foreign armies. He soon acquired the reputation of a talented military planner. By the end of 1950, however, he had to leave and was appointed Head of the General Staff's Operations Division. It was a job that did not require combat experience as much as organisational skill. Rabin, who saw himself as a military man and not an organiser of men and equipment, was disappointed and frustrated by his new appointment and he immediately asked for a transfer. But his request was refused and grudgingly he took on his new job.

A considerable amount of time had to be dedicated to one of the most pressing tasks of the new state: the housing and integration of hundred of thousands of immigrants who had flocked to the young state from Europe and the Arab countries. The newcomers varied greatly in their backgrounds. Some of them had barely survived the horrors of the Holocaust, others had fled Arab hostility and some just wanted to be part of the making and fostering of the Jewish state. Israel encouraged and welcomed the immigrants; the 'ingathering of the exiles' was one of its main aims and it needed immigrants to settle the land and thus to firmly establish its presence in all of it. But it was also aware of the potential dangers a disgruntled mass could pose to the political establishment if it should fail to be successfully integrated. Thus the army, the 'nation's emissary', as Ben Gurion liked to call it, was deployed to serve as teachers, social workers and, during the particularly harsh winter of 1951/52, when heavy rains and snowstorms brought down tents and made the already-difficult life in the camps unbearable, as engineers. Rabin, in the end, got used to his new role and later recalled the 'battle of the transit camps as, even though it was 'nonmartial', one of the 'most splendid victories'[46] of the Israeli army. But it did not leave him much time to spend with his wife and daughter Dalia, who was born in March 1950.

Rabin was an enthusiastic father but one with little time. While he was working in various positions within the army, it was Leah who raised Dalia and later their son Yuval, who was born four years later. Ironically, Rabin's children relived his childhood experience with the notable exception that his children had 'their mother at home',[47] as he once curtly replied when a journalist asked him about his rather parentless childhood and how he felt about his children who inevitably, once his career took off, had to make do with at best a part-time father. The more his public role grew, the more Leah tried to provide a stable family routine where a plate for the father was always laid on the table in the hope that he would be able to make it for dinner. Leah knew that her dedication to the children allowed him not only to throw himself 'body and soul into whatever he was doing' but that it 'compensated for his own childhood, and for the immense effort invested in whatever he did, it was the security of knowing that I was at home on a "full time job"'.[48] However, despite making a point of driving the children to school every day and spending as many weekends as possible with them, their father remained largely absent from their everyday life.

After two years of non-military operations, Rabin was offered the opportunity to study abroad for a year. Although he and Leah had only recently moved into their first home in Zahala, a suburb of Tel Aviv, he gladly accepted the offer. Unfortunately it was not the much-admired United States he was sent to, but dreary England, the home of the hated former Mandate power. Unsurprisingly, Rabin dedicated only 13 lines in his memoirs to the entire year he spent at the Royal Staff College at Camberley, a couple of miles outside of London. It was indeed a mixed experience: from a professional point of view he benefited from the part of the course covering operational planning but was extremely bored by a range of 'technical staff work' which involved such 'bizarre' exercises as 'working out a transportation timetable for an entire division'. It rightfully made him question the courses' usefulness to him, since the Israeli army did not even have 'any formation as large as a division'.[49] On a more personal level he ran into many officers who only a few years ago had been forcefully driven out of Palestine; animosity and ill-feeling between him and the representatives of the former power frequently resurfaced. Fate would also have it that the commandant of the College had been the battalion commander who had arrested him in 1946. But if Rabin was not taken by the English and their military doctrine, the British officers were equally unimpressed by the Israeli soldier, whose English was poor and whose army, at least by their standards, was a joke. Once Rabin told Leah that after he had voiced his opinion about some possible battle scenario, his instructor curtly commented that his suggestions were quite interesting and 'by the way, just how many divisions does the Israeli armoured corps have, Lieutenant-Colonel Rabin?'.[50] After the course was over, some of his classmates reportedly told their superiors that Rabin was at best suitable 'as an officer in the quartermaster corps – providing troops with clothes and food!'[51] But despite this unpleasantness Rabin applied for a two-year course at the London School of Economics. He was not much interested in economics but viewed additional time abroad as a sensible preparation for a future career in public service when he left the military. In addition, a new Chief of Staff had taken office in Israel. Rabin had gotten along well with Mordechai Makleff but less so with his successor, Moshe Dayan, a close ally of Ben Gurion. When he asked Makleff if he could extend his studies abroad, Makleff said that this was for Dayan to decide. But when Rabin met Dayan during a stopover in London, he made it clear that he wanted Rabin to return. After a brief tour of Europe he went back to Israel with no idea what his new job would be and with a sense of apprehension that the incident of the Palmach rally might not be entirely forgotten.

A Slow Rise to the Top: 1953–1963

On Rabin's return to Israel in 1953, to his great surprise Dayan asked him to head a new Training Branch at the General Headquarters. During the next three years Rabin often worked up to 18 hours a day to devise new military strategies, combat doctrines and instruction manuals for soldiers and officers. He not only standardised literature on troop training but also spread exercises throughout the IDF and developed multi-year training courses for the units. His strategic work formed the foundation for the method that would ultimately prepare the Israeli army for the next war.[52]

The dominant attitude of Israeli politicians as well as military leaders in the early 1950s was mainly determined by the belief that relations with the Arab states should be conducted via military strength and not diplomatic initiatives. The Israeli attitude towards the Arab states was greatly influenced by the negative Jewish experience in Europe, the murderous Holocaust and Arab resentment of a Jewish state in their midst. While he actively sought Western military and economic assistance, Ben Gurion insisted on Israel's independence of action and refused the Western powers any say over it. Since the Arab states refused to recognise Israel he was convinced that only military might would force them to accept the Jewish state. Together with Moshe Dayan he ordered a policy of instant reprisal should any act of aggression be committed against Israel. Especially on the Israeli–Jordanian frontier numerous 'border transgression' took place in the early 1950s and later increasingly 'personal assaults', mostly committed by Palestinians who tried to tend the fields they had been forced to abandon as a result of the war, which were met by a series of reprisal raids by the Israelis. The combination of 'being threatened with a belief in Israel's military superiority' led to military actions which were 'often intentionally aggressive'[53] and also led to border clashes with Egypt. The more assuaging approach of men like Moshe Sharett who was Foreign Minister at that time, went largely ignored and, together with all more moderate politicians, was viewed by Ben Gurion and Dayan as a liability weakening Israel's position. Moshe Dayan believed that Israel's aggressive tactics were an important tool to 'make it possible for us to maintain a high level of tension among our population and in the army. Without these actions [assaults] we would have ceased to be a combative people and without that discipline we are lost'.[54] Ben Gurion's approach to the Arab world and particular to the Palestinians was based on 'the vision of the "ancient kingdom" of the Israelites resurrected as a modern bastion of Western interests in the Middle East' a perception that was shared by many army generals who all dreamt 'of a Greater Israel . . . which they thought to achieve by exploiting the overall instability in Arab politics at the time'.[55] Furthermore Ben Gurion believed the Arab world to be intrinsically hostile, a conviction that was reinforced by the Arab states' often war-like rhetoric and promises of revenge for the defeat of 1948. By concentrating on his two fundamental perceptions, Ben Gurion overlooked that many Arab states were 'immediately after the 1948 war . . . much more committed to the peace process the UN had started and was nurturing'[56] than he was.

Thus, official peace offers by Israel, which were frequently released, purposely fell short of Arab demands since 'the main impetus for these announcements was pressure from Western powers' and they were made more with 'an eye to public consumption abroad than out of any expectation of positive response'.[57] The domestic debate was dominated by discussion of how best to deter possible Arab attacks – especially after Egypt and Syria turned to the Eastern bloc for arms – and if this should fail, how to gain greater security. The leader of the opposition, Menachem Begin, was in favour of an Israeli attack on the West Bank and the expulsion of its Palestinian population in order to regain land that he considered an integral part of the ancient Jewish homeland which he called by its biblical name of 'Judea and Samaria'. Ben Gurion, who principally tried to secure Israel's continued existence by military action rather than diplomacy, preferred to wait for the proper moment to do so, and if possible with Western backing. This opportunity presented itself in 1956. The so-called Suez Crisis, where France and Britain joined Israel in launching an attack against Egypt, had its roots in the evolving alliance between Israel and the two European states, the beginning of the Cold War and the rise of the Egyptian Gamal Abdel Nasser as the leader of Arab nationalism.

The Arabs, especially the younger generation, perceived their defeat in 1948 as a consequence of Arab inefficiency in the face of a Western-backed imperial power. They were united in their resentment of Israel and a desire for retribution. But domestic problems, coupled with the fear of Israel's military might, were more pressing than their desire for revenge. Syria, Iraq and Egypt in particular experienced political turmoil, unrest and coups which profoundly changed their political landscape. On the other hand, Britain, France and the emerging superpower America tried to counter Soviet encroachment into the strategically-important region by drawing Arab countries into military pacts which would guarantee their interests. Israel, which tried to become the West's sole strategic partner, found itself in tough competition with the Arab states, particularly when the US established cordial relations with Egypt. This was to change when Gamal Abdel Nasser came to power in 1952 in a bloodless coup. He soon became the central figure who would challenge Western regional influence, seek Arab independence and become the leader of pan-Arab nationalism. After securing his domestic position he quickly turned his attention to Egypt's relations with the West, especially its uncomfortable alliance with Britain. When Britain initiated the Baghdad Pact with Turkey, Iran, Pakistan and Iraq to recruit allies for its fight against Soviet involvement in the region, Nasser refused to join and got Syria and Jordan to do likewise. But Egypt was also in need of military assistance, especially in light of increasing Israeli raids on its territory. By 1954 Israel had concluded a lucrative arms deal with France to whom it had first turned to secretly, since neither Britain nor the US wished to openly provide Israel with weapons, since they felt that Israel was already well-equipped and did not want to alienate possible Arab allies. To avoid alignment with the West Nasser concluded an arms deal with

Czechoslovakia in 1955, which was in effect a Soviet–Egyptian one. While the Arab public welcomed his move, Britain and the US, which had tacitly sanctioned the Baghdad Pact, were anything but pleased. When Nasser attempted to build a dam across the Nile at Aswan, a key project for Egyptian economic and industrial progress as he saw it and a means to further boost his prestige at home and in the Arab world, Britain and the US decided to curb his ambitions. Thus when Nasser turned to the World Bank for financial assistance, they first attached several conditions to it and then, like the US, withdrew their support. In return and as a final act of defiance Nasser decided, to much domestic public acclaim, to nationalise the Suez Canal to use its proceeds to finance the dam. Britain reacted by calling the nationalisation 'theft and spoke in ominous terms about teaching the Egyptian president a lesson'.[58] By October 1956 Britain, France and Israel, all for their own reasons but united in their aim to put an end to Nasser's presidency, had their final excuse and attacked Egypt. While the Suez invasion was ultimately a failure for Britain and France, it proved to be quite a success for Israel. Under great pressure from the United States, who considered their military campaign to curb Nasser's power an act of deception as well of stupidity,[59] Britain and France had to withdraw their forces. It marked the end for Britain of its imperial glory and for France a fiasco which it could conveniently blame on the British.[60] Israel, on the other hand, drew a different conclusion: it had not succeeded in overthrowing Nasser nor had it been able to destroy the Egyptian forces but it had succeeded in opening the Straits of Tiran to Israeli ships, achieved a *de facto* peace along the Egyptian–Israeli border and laid the foundation for US support which at first came mainly through the lobbying efforts of American Jews. Shortly afterwards the Eisenhower doctrine came into effect which was to provide US-friendly countries with military and economic backing as long as they stayed away from the Soviet Union; Israel would become one of the main beneficiaries of this new and active policy of US interference in the Middle East.

Rabin, since spring 1956 a major-general, had been stationed in the north of Israel, heading the Northern Command. Although he said that he welcomed the change after having spent so many years on staff duty he was deeply disappointed that Dayan had put him so far away from military action even before the Suez Crisis had taken place in the south. Once Israeli attacks on Egypt had started – the closing of the Straits did not come as a surprise to him as he had already opposed Israeli withdrawal from Egyptian territory during the armistice negotiations in Rhodes – he was frustrated that his assignment forced him to watch from afar how the IDF put into practice the doctrine and manoeuvres he had painstakingly helped to develop. While Rabin was frustrated for professional reasons, Leah was annoyed for private ones. She had moved with the children to the northern port city of Haifa in order to be closer to Yitzhak, but found herself irritated with her sole occupation of looking after a baby and a toddler in a city that made her feel socially suffocated and culturally strangled. With Yitzhak on call most of the time her only companion was her sister Aviva and her children.

While Rabin was dealing with border incidents in the north, which involved the shelling of Israeli settlements, shooting incidents on both sides and Israeli naval raids in the disputed waters of the Sea of Galilee, Moshe Dayan's term as Chief of Staff came to an end. With the decision of his successor still pending, Rabin and other officers were invited by Dayan for an informal talk. Dayan spoke about the kind of successor he would expect and Rabin, against his instincts and natural pessimism, hoped that it would be him. When Rabin heard his name as a possible candidate, it seemed obvious to him 'that Dayan was hinting that my usefulness to the army had run its course and I should therefore terminate my service'.[61] A thought which was not entirely alien to any of the senior officers: they all had at one point to consider a future outside the army if they were not promoted to the highest echelon of the IDF. Rabin was not keen to do so at that moment and the idea that his army career might be nearing its end left him feel uncomfortable. Eventually, however, he came round to it and said that he was willing to continue his studies. He spoke with Dayan after the meeting and said that he would like to go to Harvard to study public administration, a subject whose practical aspects he knew inside-out thanks to his army service but had no academic grounding in. As Dayan's successor, Chaim Laskov, also approved of his plans he successfully applied to Harvard and he started to prepare to leave Israel in the summer of 1959. But as had happened in the past, it was not he himself who decided his future but an incident beyond his control: a public mobilisation exercise that got wildly out of hand. Instead of alerting only those who were to take part in the exercise, a serious blunder by the staff responsible led to a series of radio announcements that called-up the whole country without any assurances that this was just an exercise and not a genuine emergency. The embarrassing, and for the majority of Israelis quite frightening, incident was subsequently investigated and the Chief of Operations as well as the Chief of Military Intelligence found themselves relieved of duty. Chaim Laskov wanted the 37-year-old Rabin as his new Chief of Operations, the second-highest position in the IDF. To Rabin's great relief Ben Gurion, who after a brief absence from the post of Prime Minister had either entirely forgotten or altered his memories of the Palmach rally episode, agreed. Rabin remembered his unexpected promotion as 'not for the last time, I saw that we sometimes move ahead not only by virtue of our own powers but in the wake of errors committed by others'.[62]

In the following years Rabin's reputation as one of the most capable officers of the IDF grew. His phenomenal memory, ability to think strategically and analyse military problems in depth and in anticipation of things to come made him much admired by his senior colleagues and soldiers alike. His no-nonsense, matter-of-fact approach and direct speech were much appreciated on a professional level. However, he had little patience for people whose thoughts and ideas he considered irrelevant and, contrary to his general reserve, he did not hesitate to voice his opinions loudly and clearly. In particular his shyness and his inability to share his feelings with others apart from his wife, did not allow him to form warm or intimate relationships with any of the people he worked with. Even his closest aides, who appreciated his concern whenever they had a serious private problem to deal with, knew little about the inner life of the man who often spent more time with them than with his family.

Not only did he travel widely during the following years to learn more about the latest military equipment and techniques, but he also felt for the first time that his new post awarded him the chance to 'deal comprehensively with every facet of the defence forces'[63] which he was determined would master future wars. He was particularly concerned about the involvement of the Soviet Union in the equipment and training of the armies of the Arab states. Thus he insisted that the IDF incorporate Soviet-style doctrines and procedures into its training. He had already streamlined the literature for training troops and had methodically spread it throughout the IDF when he headed the Training Branch in order to prepare it for war. But it was during his tenure as Chief of Operations that he left one of his most defining marks on the Israeli army.

One of the re-emerging themes was the question from whom Israel should try to acquire weapons. It had for many years relied on French arms but Rabin feared that Israel's 'almost total dependence' on France had been 'imprudent'. He considered reliance on only one supplier as 'too risky' – he was afraid that France would withhold arms when it disagreed politically with Israel – and feared that 'the scope of French arms manufacture and the existent terms of credit were no match for the massive flow of Soviet arms to the Arab states'.[64] Israel had for many years, despite France's waning geopolitical weight especially after 1956, relied heavily on its weapons. This was due to the fact that Israel's efforts in the late 1940s to secure greater US support had born little fruit, that it was obvious that Israel could not manage alone, and France was a willing partner. Rabin, who was known for his admiration of nearly all things American, always had the US in mind when he thought about an able, powerful military and political partner for Israel. The numerous trips to the States which he undertook in those years only strengthened his belief that American weapons were the answer to Israel's arms problem. But it was an assessment which was not shared by the man who had been in charge of organising arms for Israel for many years: Deputy Defence Minister Shimon Peres.

Rabin and Peres could not have been more different. Not a 'sabra', a native, like Rabin, Peres, born in 1923 in Poland, arrived in Palestine at the age of 11. While studying business, he had developed a taste for politics and soon joined the youth movement of the Mapai party and became its secretary in 1943. Around that time he also changed his name from Persky to Peres. But his political career took off only after a chance encounter with Ben Gurion. The 60-year-old was on the lookout for potential new leaders and found in Peres a talented man and eager follower. In 1947 Peres joined him at the headquarters of the Hagana. When Peres was offered promotion to the rank of major, he refused and instead was put in charge of acquiring weapons for the coming war by Ben Gurion. It was a position Peres would skilfully occupy for the next few years. Despite his steady rise within the party, his lack of military credentials, the 'black hole in his biography',[65] made him suspect in the eyes of the establishment to which Rabin belonged. Like others, Rabin never really trusted the shtetl boy from the Diaspora. But they were not only complete opposites in their upbringing and careers, their characters were also at odds: 'the military man did not trust the apparatchik, the intellectual mocked the simpleton, the showman scoffed the grafter, and the father of the model family was, without any doubt, envious of the bon viveur'.[66] Even though Rabin downplayed his first major argument with Peres as collateral damage caused by the clash of two schools of thought – one favouring an alliance with Europe, the other one with the United States – their rivalry was to dominate and often cripple Israeli politics for many years to come. As far as their first disagreement went Rabin eventually won and America became Israel's main ally and provider not only of defensive but also increasingly of offensive weaponry.

On the Way to War and Victory:
1964–1967

On 1 January 1964 Yitzhak Rabin, 'a worthy candidate'[67] in his own words, became Chief of Staff. His appointment to the highest post in the Israeli army did not go smoothly and was marred by political and personal infighting. Ben Gurion wanted to prevent Rabin's appointment – possibly remembering his past disobedience or simply preferring a political ally – and had favoured another candidate, Zvi Zur. Rabin was angered by what he perceived as Ben Gurion's personal vendetta and the excuses he gave for having chosen Zur with whom Rabin did not get along. But then Ben Gurion resigned again in the summer of 1963 and Levi Eshkol replaced him as Prime Minister and Defence Minister. Eshkol approved of Rabin, and Ben Gurion, shortly before leaving office, showed some consideration and reportedly gave his blessing to the appointment after all. Rabin was convinced that it was actually Peres who was behind the farce and that he had 'pressed for my replacement' because he, Rabin 'was a thorn in his side' and thus had unduly 'fomented personal conflicts to place his adversaries under pressure'.[68]

He began his term as Israel's seventh Chief of Staff among growing external and internal tensions. The decade after the Suez campaign had witnessed a change of regimes in many Arab states, often bringing radical groups to power which frequently proved to be unpopular. Egypt and particularly Syria were seeking an alliance that was viewed by Israel with suspicion. Border clashes between the latter and Israel grew in frequency and ferocity during the mid-1960s. The most decisive factor in the escalation of rhetoric and action was Israel's plan to go ahead with an irrigation project in the North which it had started to plan in the 1950s and which drew heavily on the shared water of Syria and Israel, the Sea of Galilee. The United States, aware of the importance of water in the region and its potential for causing conflict, developed a water-sharing plan which would have divided the water between Israel, Syria, Jordan and Lebanon to ease the mounting friction. In response, the Arab states called a summit in January and September 1964 where they rejected the arrangement, fearing that acceptance of the plan would equal recognition of Israel, something they absolutely refused. Instead they decided on 'collective Arab military preparations . . .[which would constitute] the ultimate practical means for the liquidation of Israel'[69] to stop the scheme while developing their own plan to limit Israel's ability to divert water. In addition border infiltrations from Syria into Israel became more frequent, and were mainly carried out by Palestinian guerrilla groups, chiefly Fatah, the Palestinian National Liberation Movement. It had been founded in the late 1950s at informal gatherings of disaffected Palestinians, among them Yassir Arafat. The movement insisted that 'armed struggle' was the only way to resist the Jewish state and to 'liberate Palestine'. Fatah believed in the unification of all Palestinians as a prerequisite for the desired liberation of Palestine. It was particularly opposed to the attempts by Arab states to settle the Arab–Israeli conflict by political means. Only after decades of violence against the Israeli state and its people did Fatah arrive at a two-state solution and accept that fighting would not achieve anything.

The Israeli army, under the command of Rabin, reacted with fierce, yet often symbolic, reprisals. The situation further escalated when Rabin ordered an attack on the village of Samu on the Jordanian-controlled West Bank. Initially intended to deter civilians from supporting Fatah, it got out of control and Rabin came under criticism for unnecessarily aggravating the situation, particularly since Jordan did not approve of Palestinian raids into Israel out of fear of direct military confrontation with the superior Israeli army. As a result, Rabin stepped-up his reprisal attacks on Syria, which he correctly accused of aiding Fatah, thus making it a legitimate target in his eyes. Rabin was much more willing to employ force then the Israeli Prime Minister. Even though Rabin and Eshkol shared a good working relationship, with Eshkol relying on Rabin's sound military and political judgement, the Samu raid and a bellicose comment in an interview in 1966 for the army newspaper *B'Machane*, where he said that Israel should fight not only those who carried out the raids but also strike against the 'regimes which support those acts',[70] caused friction between them. Rabin on the other hand praised Eshkol not so much for his politics but for his 'historic decision to intensify our campaign to break into the American arms market'.[71] While Israel threatened in the lead-up to its independence day to overthrow the Syrian regime by military force if attacks from its territory continued, Egypt, which by then had successfully concluded a military defence pact with Syria, joined the confrontational rhetoric and after having received – albeit false – Soviet intelligence on alleged Israeli troop movements towards Sinai, itself moved troops there and eventually closed the Straits. It was less a move against Israel but aimed to secure Nasser the position as the leader of the Arab world. Israel however took his move as an act of aggression and called up its reservists amongst an atmosphere of isolation and deepening economic and political crisis.

Economically Israel suffered from a combination of inflation, trade deficit and high levels of consumption that necessitated a policy of economic slowdown by means of highly unpopular cuts in public spending. Politically the country experienced a leadership crisis. Eshkol was not only pressured by senior generals to seize the moment and, by a surprise attack, enhance Israel's chance to make territorial gains that would enable the country to achieve defendable borders, but was also attacked by his political rivals, namely Ben Gurion, Shimon Peres and Moshe Dayan, who tried to undermine his authority while furthering their own. Internal peace and public confidence was only restored after Eshkol agreed to a national unity government with Moshe Dayan as Defence Minister and the inclusion of the leader of the right-wing party, Menachem Begin. But not only Eshkol's stature suffered, his Chief of Staff too endured moments of waning self-confidence during this period of waiting which to him was nothing less than the 'the gravest situation Israel had known since the War of Independence'.[72] Regardless of having developed the IDF into a professional and excellently-prepared army which, he was convinced, could win any war without question, he was weighed down by the heavy responsibility, exhausted by the nerve-wracking waiting and the adverse impact of his mobilisation orders in response to Egypt's closure of the Straits. He decided to see Ben Gurion, who despite his official retirement was still was an authoritative figure, for an informal talk. Instead of reassuring him, however, the old man accused Rabin of having made a great mistake that had created an untenable situation which increased the chances of war and for which he, Rabin, had to bear all the consequences.[73] In old film footage of those weeks one can see a tense, jittery and chain-smoking Chief of Staff on visits to the troops. The overwhelming burden proved too much and he suffered a breakdown. Rabin later denied that he succumbed to the pressure and collapsed but attributed his enforced rest, ordered by Leah and recommended by his doctor, to a 'combination of tension, exhaustion, and the enormous amounts of cigarette smoke'.[74] After just one day he was back, waiting for Eshkol to order an attack, believing that Egypt had provided the *casus belli* and the 'ball was in our court'.[75] Eshkol, however, still wanted American endorsement of any military moves. But since the Americans were convinced that Egypt had no intention of going to war, they did not approve of hostile Israeli actions. Only after the Israelis learned in early June of Nasser's plan to gain American silence concerning the blocking of the Straits, a plan to which Israel feared America was likely to agree, did the cabinet approve on 4 June to attack Egypt the next day. Rabin would later say that he did not 'believe that Nasser wanted war. The two divisions he sent into Sinai on May 14th would not have been enough to unleash an offensive against Israel. He knew it and we knew it'.[76] Yet, the official line was that Egypt's closure of the Straits of Tiran gave Israel the right to act. Only much later Menachem Begin, when prime minister, stated: 'we must be honest with ourselves. We decided to attack him . . . [in order to] take the initiative, attack the enemy, drive him back, and thus assure the security and the future of the nation'.[77] Yet, no matter that some Israelis saw the June war as a continuation of the war of 1948, Israel had 'no master plan for territorial aggrandisement' and its territorial aims 'were defined not in advance but in response to developments on the battlefield'.[78] And there were plenty of those.

The following war lasted only six days and resulted in a tremendous victory for Israel. The IDF under the command of Rabin completely destroyed the Egyptian air force within the first three hours of the war and by 9 June, to the tune of the popular Israeli song 'Nasser is waiting for Rabin', it reached the Suez Canal. After Jordan began to shell Israel, the army, following Rabin's conviction that any war, since 'Israel lacked strategic depth . . . must be fought on enemy's territory and that enemy forces must be defeated as quickly as humanly possible',[79] took one West Bank village after the other with startling swiftness. In the north Israel captured the Golan Heights overlooking the contested waters of the Sea of Galilee from Syria. Most importantly, Israel took East Jerusalem which had been under Jordanian rule since 1948 and was separated by barbed wire from the Jewish West. It was a magical moment for a people whose holiest site stood in the Old City: the Western Wall. Rabin and Dayan entered the Old City through the Lion Gate, Rabin feeling overwhelmed by the excitement. For years he had 'secretly harboured the dream' that he would play a part 'in restoring the Western Wall to the Jewish people'. Despite his secular upbringing he felt not only 'privileged' but also wondered whether he would ever feel 'quite the same peak of elation'[80] again when he finally reached the old temple walls. Regardless of all his heartfelt elation he remained cautious. He immediately sensed the potential problems the territorial gains brought in the long run: he worried whether the army – not used to thinking in terms of distances covering hundred of kilometres – would be able to secure the new borders and he anticipated the problems the occupation of about a million Palestinians would cause. He did not call them by their name, merely referring to them by the general term 'Arabs', but he conceded that they were 'human beings' that had 'to make a living, eat, receive services, and be permitted freedom of movement' and he was 'conscious of the fact that they would be subject to the temptation to harm us'.[81]

But his was a lone voice. The overwhelming victory, encapsulated in the apt name of 'The Six Day War', as the war of 1967 became known, created a truly delirious atmosphere. The fear of external threat and fearful anticipation – so prevalent only a couple of days before – had given way to collective rejoicing which kept the vast majority of Israelis in a dreamlike state. The army naturally received the greatest popular adulation. Although it was Rabin who had prepared Israel's triumph, it was Moshe Dayan, the acting Defence Minister, who became the hero of the war. Rabin never explicitly said whether he was disappointed by the public's reaction but many years later, in a television interview during which he was asked how he generally awarded the credit after a successful military operation, he replied that the credit should always be given to the one who would have been held responsible if the operation had failed. There was little doubt whose job would have been on the line if Israel had suffered defeat in the summer of 1967. During a ceremony at the Hebrew University in Jerusalem shortly after the war, where Rabin was awarded an Honorary Doctorate in way of compensation, he gave a sombre speech, noticeable lacking in the vocabulary of victory: '[the soldiers'] triumph is marred by grief and shock, and there are some who cannot rejoice at all. The men in the front lines saw with their own eyes not only the glory of victory but also its cost: their comrades fallen besides them, soaked in blood. And I know the terrible price the enemy paid has also deeply moved many of our men. Is it because neither their teaching nor their experience has ever accustomed the Jewish people to exult in conquest and victory, that they receive them with such mixed feelings?'.[82] In the end and despite Dayan reaping most of the acclaim, Rabin's image as a victorious soldier was firmly planted in the back of Israelis' minds.

A Change of Battlefields:
1968–1973

The Six Day War was unquestionably the peak of Rabin's military career. Faced with the natural end of his term as Chief of Staff, he had been already contemplating his future outside the military before the war. Many friends had urged him to enter politics but he rejected the idea, if only for the moment. He had other plans and they centred on the post of Israel's Ambassador to the United States. He was confident that his military and political background would provide him with the necessary skills on this unfamiliar ground; the thought of having to endure endless small talk peppered with meaningless exchanges of pleasantries at countless compulsory cocktail parties apparently did not worry him.[83] But it worried Levi Eshkol: he said he nearly fell off his chair when first being confronted with Rabin's request. His mind was made up and he lobbied for the appointment relentlessly and in the end successfully, despite an array of better-versed diplomatic competitors. Rabin's main motivation in becoming Israel's man in Washington was his understanding of America's role in the world and Israel's need for its military and political support. He wanted not only arms to maintain Israel's edge over the Arab armies – he firmly believed that what was good for the army was good for the country – but also to co-ordinate the two countries' policies. Shortly before he left for the United States he presented a blueprint of his objectives to the Foreign Ministry which outlined close military and economic co-operation between the US and Israel. He intended to prove to America that Soviet involvement in the Middle East and its support for Arab states must end and that Israel and the Arabs had to settle their dispute without Superpower intervention. He also sought to make America understand that its interests were in fact the same as Israel's and thus justify a steady flow of arms which would help both countries to assert themselves.

The slightly-reduced Rabin family arrived in Washington in February 1968. Dalia had stayed behind in Israel to finish high school and then to do her compulsory military service. Separating the family was difficult, as Rabin was particularly close to Dalia. She had been a sickly child, fighting a heart condition that had often forced her into hospital for lengthy periods during which Rabin tried his best to free himself from work to spend as much time as possible with her. Yuval would eventually grow so homesick that he envied his sister's situation: parentless but at least at home.

The America Rabin found upon his arrival was a country caught up in external and internal turmoil. The administration headed by Lyndon Johnson, who had become president after the assassination of John F Kennedy in 1963, was sympathetic to the splendid victor of the last Arab–Israeli confrontation. Yet his benevolence was in part the result of the enormous support Israel enjoyed among the influential Jewish constituency in the

United States. Israel's position of no return to the borders of 1948 and no return of any occupied territory without full peace with the Arabs was viewed with scepticism and the expectation was for an eventual Israeli withdrawal on the basis of UN Resolution 242, the so-called 'land for peace' resolution. This resolution, stressing 'the inadmissibility of the acquisition of territory by war'[84] called on all parties to seek a comprehensive settlement that should be based on two principles: Israel's withdrawal from territory occupied in the 1967 war and respect for all states in the region to live in peace and within secure borders. It also acknowledged the necessity to find a just solution to the problem of the Palestinian refugees. Yet, since the Americans blocked an attempt to put the word 'the' before the word 'territories' from which Israel was expected to withdraw, the specific territory in question remained unclear and open to interpretation. However, it was not only that the wording was unclear, but also, as some critics noted, it implied a recognition of Israel's sovereignty within the armistice lines of 1948 – meant to be only temporary – and thus acceptance of Israel's territorial gains during its War of Independence. Secondly the resolution was a recommendation only and not binding on all UN member states. Israel, Egypt, Jordan and Lebanon accepted the resolution, but Syria and the Palestinians rejected it. The former encouraged renewed raids by Palestinians against Israel and the latter insisted that they had been marginalised as a non-political issue thus being denied the right to sovereignty in their homeland. Unsurprisingly, nothing came of the mission of the UN emissary Gunnar Jarring to persuade all parties and the Arab position reinforced the Israeli one, insisting on keeping the territories as a security buffer.

Rabin trod carefully during his first months. He acquainted himself with the country, endured a first round of diplomatic receptions and familiarised himself with the situation in the Far East where the Americans were 'hopelessly bogged down in the Vietnam conflict',[85] and, as the highly-decorated Israeli general noted with incredulity, obviously without an 'overall plan for winning'.[86] 1968 was also an election year which provided Rabin with a taste of the American way of popular political decision-making: television, which Israel did not have at that time. It was through this unfamiliar medium that he learned that Johnson had no intention of seeking a second term in office. Rabin was invited to the house of an American journalist in order to watch the President's speech to the nation. While the other guests assumed that this was a mere tactical move, Rabin immediately thought about the possible political implications it might have. Even though Johnson disagreed with Israel's intention to hold on to the newly-acquired territories, he still approved a massive shipment of Phantom and Skyhawk fighter jets. With the election under way, America experienced severe internal disturbances including anti-war demonstrations, race riots and the assassinations of Martin Luther King and Robert F Kennedy. To the 'new and inexperienced ambassador' the situation appeared 'depressingly grave'.[87] He feared that the external as well as internal upheavals might undermine America's role in international politics and thus endanger his plans. But the election of Richard Nixon caused him cautious optimism. The two men had already met two years previously at a formal dinner in Tel Aviv. They had talked about Israel's situation and Rabin had quickly gotten the feeling that he was talking to someone who was well-disposed towards Israel. Shortly after Nixon took office Rabin started his campaign to get through essential arms deals and to convince the President that Israel's interest were compatible with his own. While Rabin made progress in gradually turning the American–Israeli relationship into a close strategic alliance, the situation in the Middle East remained serious.

After the untimely death from cancer of Levi Eshkol, Golda Meir, a 71-year-old woman of nearly equal ill-health succeeded him. She was by nature and style the complete opposite of the more conciliatory and assuaging Eshkol and revealed a 'remarkable capacity for simplifying complex problems'. But she shared with the late Eshkol the conviction that Israel would only concede territory for a comprehensive peace agreement and insisted that the pre-1967 borders were null and void. In practice her policy amounted to preservation of the *status quo* and the avoidance of political risks.[88] It fitted the popular mood in a country that was polarised about the question what to do with the newly occupied lands. Whereas some happily embraced the Jewish return to ancient territory, namely the West Bank ('Samaria and Judea'), others, fearing for the Jewish character of Israel, wished either to use them as bargaining chips in future peace negotiations or to get rid of them immediately. However, the ever-increasing influence of the military successfully prevented a political solution since any political agreement was deemed to jeopardise Israel's security.

The failure to settle the dispute diplomatically eventually led to the Egyptian–Israeli War of Attrition, beginning in spring 1969. Rabin backed military action and accepted that force was the only way to show the Arabs that Israel would not be pressured into concessions, either territorial or political. In the midst of this military escalation, however, the American

Secretary of State William Rogers, who had a different opinion from the rest of the Administration, came forward with a peace initiative, the Rogers Plan. The State Department had previously attempted a more even-handed approach towards the conflict and had enlisted Soviet support for it. The initiative called for a return of nearly all land, Arab recognition of Israel and the definition of secure borders. Rogers hoped that the plan could be agreed upon by Russia and the United States first and then be presented to France and Britain who would first endorse it and then allow the UN emissary Gunnar Jarring to convince the Israelis and the Arabs. The more militant Arab regimes immediately denounced the initiative, but it received considerable praise, if not without qualification, from Egypt and Jordan. Egypt particularly, albeit supportive of the part which specified Israel withdrawal, feared that the Rogers Plan would merely constitute a separate accord between Israel and Egypt rather than the comprehensive regional settlement they wanted.

The Israelis, including their American Ambassador, had no prior knowledge of the Rogers Plan and were equally surprised and shocked. The plan came also at a very inconvenient time: national elections were due. The Labour Party presented to the Israelis their post-election plan which firmly rested on keeping the Golan Heights, the formerly Egyptian Sharm al-Sheikh, Gaza and some unspecified parts of the West Bank, which clearly ran counter to Resolution 242 and thus the Rogers Plan. Rabin had several objections to the Plan: he generally disliked the UN, was against any settlement imposed from outside – especially if it was brokered between the US and Russia – and he did not get on with Rogers whom he accused of having limited knowledge of the Middle East. Rogers, in turn, abhorred Rabin's humourless candour. Meir at once ordered Rabin, who considered the plan a 'disaster',[89] to return to Israel for consultations. Together they explored several avenues as to how best to undermine the project while displaying an ostensibly positive attitude in public so as not jeopardise American arms shipments. Rabin was close to Meir who had known and worked with his mother and who was as much taken with his intelligence as, at times, by motherly feelings for him. Upon his return Rabin defied Rogers with a strongly-worded rejection. Getting nowhere with the Secretary of State, Rabin turned to other key members in the American administration and soon found a particularly close ally in Henry Kissinger, the National Security Adviser. The two men regularly met for lunch and sometimes even under 'cloak-and-dagger'[90] circumstance to discuss without unnecessary embellishments their pragmatic understanding of international politics, their mistrust of the Soviets and their attempts to show to the Arabs that being on good terms with America was the key to success.

At the same time, and in accordance with his cardinal belief that a strong Israel would inevitably improve America's standing and therefore be supported by it, he recommended that Israel 'escalate . . . military pressure on Egypt'.[91] To this end Israel not only launched attacks across the border but penetrated deeply into Egyptian territory. Israel's belligerent stand and its refusal to agree to a temporary ceasefire, an idea first suggested by Nasser and therefore rejected by Israel, had the reverse effect. Nasser turned to Moscow for assistance and the military balance shifted in favour of Egypt. Rabin was still sure that the raids had been necessary and thought that more pressure should be brought to bear on Egypt, even when, as a result, Israel's need for American arms had increased by 1970.

His aggressiveness and attempts to shape and decide Israel's foreign policy from Washington irked Israel's Foreign Minister, Abba Eban. Eban was much more conciliatory than Rabin and disliked his increasingly independent actions; especially since Rabin hardly bothered to disguise his disdain for career diplomats like Eban. In an interview in May 1972, barely concealing his distaste, he said that 'Israel's successful relations with the US were entirely due to him and his Embassy Staff' and not the work of the Foreign Office which only produced people 'concerned with the niceties of protocol and etiquette' rather 'than with the important side of diplomacy'.[92]

But Rabin had to concede that Israel's intransigence had in fact backfired and left it in a 'pretty bleak position' where 'worse was' still 'to come':[93] the Rogers Plan B. It was again based on Resolution 242, called for a withdrawal from occupied territory and a three-month ceasefire between Egypt and Israel followed by – unspecified – border negotiations. The Israeli cabinet reluctantly approved the plan but only after Nixon assured them that he would continue his economic and military assistance. The ceasefire went into effect in August 1970 but was soon broken by Egypt with Russian help; in response Israel suspended any peace talks, leaving the overall impression it was the major obstacle to peace.

However, several developments within the region helped Rabin to present Israel as the principal and most important ally of the United States. One was the death of Nasser. His successor, Anwar al Sadat, faced the devastating results of Nasser's failed economic policies and was forced to seek an accommodation with Israel and especially with the United States whose economic aid Egypt desperately needed. But the more unsettling and in the end decisive factor that was to position Israel alongside America were developments in Jordan.

The Palestinian Fatah, under the new leadership of Yassir Arafat, had already set out in the mid-1960s to ignite a popular revolutionary war of liberation in the West Bank. However, Israel's occupation and the lack of support among local Palestinians necessitated a retreat to Jordan. There, the Palestinian refugee camps proved a fertile recruitment pool and soon Fatah launched new campaigns against Israel. By 1969 the Palestinian militia was formally incorporated into the official political body of the Palestinians, the Palestinian Liberation Organisation (PLO). The PLO had been formed during the Arab summit in 1964. Its establishment was mainly aimed at containing the frustration of the Palestinians who still waited for the fulfilment of Arab promises to return them to their homeland by military victory, and to co-opt Palestinian military groups which tried to force such a confrontation. At the beginning, most Palestinian militant and guerrilla groups shunned from the PLO, judging it to be a mere puppet of other Arab states. But the situation changed after the war of June 1967. The Arab states were discredited and so were the PLO leaders. Slowly the guerrilla groups, with their emphasis on popular armed resistance, became dominant in the PLO. In 1968 the PLO charter was amended and its emphasis changed: Zionism was unequivocally rejected and so was the partition of Palestine. Judaism was termed a mere religion and not a basis for an independent nationality and the PLO called for the 'total liberation of Palestine' independent from the Arab states, whose intervention was rejected. By 1969 the guerrilla groups were in the majority and they selected Yassir Arafat as the first elected head of the PLO Executive Committee.

By 1970 the PLO, relatively undisturbed by Jordan, had not only used that country as a convenient base to launch attacks on Israel proper (from about 100 attacks on military targets in 1967 to more than 2,000 in 1970),[94] but constituted a state within a state and thus posed a threat to King Hussein whose authority the PLO challenged more and more. Historically, Jordan and the Palestinians were closely linked: after 1967, when Transjordan annexed the West Bank and reconstituted itself as the Kingdom of Jordan, parts of Palestine fell within Jordanian jurisdiction. As a result about two-thirds of the Jordanian population were Palestinians. Furthermore Jordan, unlike Egypt, Syria and Lebanon where Palestinians had also fled, offered the refugees full and unconditional citizenship. Whereas some Palestinians benefited considerably from this decision, others felt like second-class citizens since Jordan clearly favoured the East Bank economically and politically, and began an internal migration from the West to the East Bank. Particularly the hundred of thousands of Palestinian refugees, who still lived mainly in camps and were barely integrated into Jordanian society, were bitter and disappointed and their resentment strengthened the appeal of Palestinian guerrilla groups. By September 1970 King Hussein decided to act. He was not only afraid of being dragged into a major military confrontation with Israel due to Palestinian raids launched from his kingdom, but also felt beleaguered by the discontented Palestinian masses and the ever-expanding autonomy of the PLO which blatantly challenged his authority by setting up armed patrols, exercising control over the refugee camps, organising mass demonstrations and provoking armed clashes with the Jordanian army. His former hesitancy and unwillingness to enter into an open conflict with the Palestinians came to end after a radical Palestinian guerrilla group, the Popular Front for the Liberation of Palestine (PFLP) – a group that was inspired by Latin American revolutionary ideology and which actively tried to topple what they considered to be reactionary Arab regimes – not only made two attempts on his life but also hijacked several planes, holding passengers hostage and demanding the release of Palestinian prisoners held in Europe. Even though the PLO condemned those actions and suspended the PFLP, the development posed an open challenge King Hussein could not ignore. On 17 September 1970, he ordered an all-out attack on Palestinian camps, the PLO headquarters and guerrilla bases.

In aid of the Palestinians, Syrian tanks invaded Jordan and the situation was about to escalate. In Israel, Golda Meir, who was sympathetic to Hussein's dilemma and felt equally threatened by Palestinian nationalism – no matter how assertively she claimed that there was no Palestinian people as such – assured the King that, if need be, Israel would back him militarily. This decision led to an eventual cooling-down of the overall situation and enabled Hussein to get rid of the PLO in what became known to the Palestinians as 'Black September', bringing their presence in Jordan to an end in a turning point in the PLO's development. But those developments aside, the mere fact that the Jordanian–Palestinian clash remained a local one was ample proof of Israel's deterrent power; a fact that did not go unnoticed in America. And by mid-1971 the Rogers Plan was finally abandoned. Israel's unwillingness to withdraw to the pre-1967 borders, even though Sadat agreed to enter a peace agreement with Israel which would have included Egypt's recognition of the Jewish state, brought all talks to a halt. Neither Nixon nor Kissinger, much to the pleasure of Rabin – who continuously received support for Israel's position in talks with both men – put any pressure on Israel. This was in part due to Nixon's desire not to upset Jewish Americans whose votes he needed if he wanted to secure a second term in office but also with the usefulness of Israel in the on-going Cold War.

Nixon's re-election occurred near the end of Rabin's diplomatic career. He still considered diplomacy as war by different means and even after four years diplomatic reticence was a skill he never fully embraced. In June 1972, a couple of months before the election, the *Washington Post* reported an interview which Rabin had given to Israeli Radio and where he barely disguised his preference for Nixon: 'While we appreciate the support in the forms we are getting from one camp, we must prefer the support in the form of deeds which we are getting from the other'.[95] At the same time as Embassy staff were at pains to explain his – intentional – slip of the tongue as being the result of his still imperfect English, Rabin himself wrote in a letter to Leah that she should 'pay no attention to the despicable reports in the papers! They are all envious of my success and they'll try any kind of smear . . . The bottom line – I am happy about my part in US–Israel relations so far'.[96]

Rabin's final day as ambassador was 11 March 1973. The American magazine *Newsweek* called him 'one of the most effective envoys in Washington' and another journalist noted that 'no other diplomat in recent years here has been attacked so often for displaying such a noticeable lack of diplomacy'.[97] Rabin could not care less: he had achieved what he had set out to do and had shown the Americans that Israel was a worthwhile partner.

From Staggering Rise to Startling Fall: 1973–1977

R abin returned to Israel amidst speculation as to what his new assignment would be. While still in Washington, he had said he would like to stand as a Labour candidate for the next Knesset elections and there had been various rumours concerning a possible cabinet post. That he would be part of the Labour party, in whatever position the party would choose, was to him self-evident: 'I was raised in a proletarian home and I was educated in the values of the Labour Movement. There can be no cause – and surely no career – which would bring me to change places'.[98] Rabin had been given a safe ticket for the upcoming elections. That autumn he was diligently campaigning, renewing old acquaintances, making new ones and experiencing a 'crash course in local political ways and byways',[99] when war suddenly broke out.

It was Friday, 5 October 1973 and the eve of the holiest day in the Jewish year. Yuval wanted to spend the Day of Atonement with his parents but received an urgent call to report back to his unit immediately. At the same time Dalia's husband was put on alert. Rabin was surprised and worried but did not believe that war was imminent. After all, he had found upon his homecoming a country that was as 'self-confident . . . as befits a country far removed from the possibility of war';[100] an assessment that was shared by many Israeli leaders, notably Israel's Defence Minister Moshe Dayan. He too did not envision any major confrontation for years to come and confidently proclaimed that Israel's military superiority would last for a decade. But the next day, when public life was completely suspended for the holiday, air raid sirens alerted the unsuspecting public that the fourth Arab–Israeli war had broken out. It should not, however, have been a surprise: Sadat, frustrated that nothing had come from the Rogers Plan and that Israel was still occupying Egyptian territory with no sign of relinquishing it, was under pressure from a disgruntled Egyptian public who had to shoulder the burden of defence without any obvious results. He was convinced that only another war would compel the superpowers, mainly the United States, to exert pressure on Israel to return to the negotiating table. Already in 1971 he had proclaimed that 'there is no longer any hope for a peaceful solution. Our decision is to fight'.[101] His conviction was reinforced when the Labour Party adopted a political platform that made any solution of the conflict based on UN Resolution 242 impossible and approved of Jewish settlements in the occupied territories.

The war, which the Israelis named after the day it broke out, Yom Kippur, lasted 17 days and resulted, after heavy losses, fierce fighting and surprisingly effective Arab attacks, in a bitter victory for Israel. The joint Egyptian and Syrian attacks took the Israelis completely by surprise and only after heavy losses and – initially refused – critical assistance from the

United States in the form of massive airlifts of arms could Israel, which at one point considered accepting calls for a ceasefire, improve its position and turn the war into victory.

For Rabin it was the first military confrontation he was not directly involved in. During the first days he went with the Chief of Staff David Elazar on several visits to the front but apart from occasionally giving advice he was not involved in any decision-making. Instead he embarked on an 'emergency-loan campaign . . . an ideal job for an ex-ambassador' on behalf of Israel's Finance Minister but he did so 'without much enthusiasm'.[102] To Leah he said 'in wars, personal fates are determined. In this war, my fate will be determined as well because I am not there. Where will I be when this is all over?'[103] But he needn't have worried: in the end his lack of involvement in the war was to his benefit.

The Yom Kippur War left the Israelis deeply traumatised. Despite their victory the obviously flawed assessments of their military and political leadership and the heavy human and financial losses created an atmosphere of vulnerability and destroyed their army's aura of invincibility. US–Israeli relations were also tested. The United States had hoped that Egyptian advances at the beginning of the war would make Israel open to a changed basis for future peace negotiations and initially had withheld arms deliveries to that end. By then Kissinger had come to the conclusion that total reliance on Israel as the sole ally of America in the Middle East might have been a mistake. As a result, Rabin, who had been sent to the US in November to secure aid for the war, had to inform Golda Meir that the Americans, following a Soviet request, insisted on a peace settlement that would satisfy all parties and wanted an international conference in Geneva based on the

Security Council Resolution 338 that called for the implementation of Resolution 242 and a 'just and durable peace'.[104]

At about the same time Israel went to the polls. Yet again, and despite growing public dissatisfaction, Labour emerged once more as the dominant political force. Golda Meir was about to present her new cabinet when she instead tendered her resignation on 10 April. A commission had been set up to investigate the actions of the military and political leadership before and after the war. The so-called Agranat Commission had absolved her government of blame and in its place named the Chief of Staff as the sole culprit. But the public did not accept its findings and called for the political leadership to accept responsibility; Meir eventually gave in to the pressure. Her most likely successor was Pinhas Sapir, the Finance Minister, but he declined and in the end there were only two candidates left: Shimon Peres and Yitzhak Rabin. Several factors worked in the end in favour of Rabin: Sapir made no secret of the fact that he preferred Rabin, Golda Meir had, shortly before her resignation, tipped him as Moshe Dayan's successor and according to a public opinion poll the people also favoured him. Rabin himself did not believe at first that he stood a chance: it was too obvious that he was a political novice with little experience in domestic affairs. But by a margin of 44 votes he won the ballot against Peres and started his term as the first Israeli-born Prime Minister, who had risen from the ranks of the army rather than those of the Labour Party, on 3 June 1974.

Rabin was stunned by his unexpected victory but soon faced the difficult reality of his new job: putting together a government. To his deep regret 'an Israeli Prime Minister is not free to nominate the ministers of his choice. The question of whether or not he will be capable of working with them –

like his opinion of their suitability for specific posts – carries no weight in our form of democracy', instead 'the other coalition partners decide who is to represent them in the cabinet' and thus the Rafi Party, a faction of Labour founded by Ben Gurion, decided on Shimon Peres as Defence Minister. Rabin neither deemed Peres qualified – 'he had never fought in the army and his expertise in arms purchasing did not make up for that lack of experience'[105] – nor particularly trustworthy. He remembered only too well a lunch invitation from Peres during their contest for the leadership. Rabin recalled Peres' promise to hold a fair competition whereby the best man should win and the other one accept his defeat gracefully. Rabin was suspicious of Peres' true motives but had agreed. Shortly before the decisive vote was about to be cast, Rabin learned of a newspaper article that referred to his breakdown shortly before the 1967 War, portraying him as a weakling once the going got tough. The article was based on documents belonging to Ezer Weizmann, Chief of Operations in 1967. Rabin had called him as he had done Ben Gurion, and asked whether he had really, as suggested by Ben Gurion, caused the current predicament and whether he should resign from his post. Weizmann, according to Rabin, talked him convincingly out of any thought of resignation. Naturally, Rabin immediately suspected someone in the Labour Party of being behind the untimely publication of Weizmann's refreshed memory. And he believed this person to be none other than Peres. In his memoirs he wrote that he remembered Weizmann saying, that even though he was not a friend of Labour he was 'a friend of Peres'.[106] While the accusation proved meaningless, Rabin and his aides suffered tense moments following the article's publication and he never forgave Peres for his campaign against him.

The press and public welcomed his election, despite his noticeable problems in forming a workable government. He faced not only the opposition of Golda Meir who, despite her initial encouragement of his candidacy, refused to support him further probably out of bitterness concerning her political fate. Pinhas Sapir too rejected co-operation and declined his offer to remain Finance Minister, and his preferred choice for Defence Minister, his mentor Yigal Allon, had to make way for Peres, who said that the Rafi Party would not support his cabinet if he was not given the defence portfolio. In the end he managed to organise a wafer-thin Parliamentary majority of one vote. Only after the entry of the National Religious Party into the coalition a year later did he enjoy a more stable majority.

His main objectives during his premiership were to influence the course and outcome of political negotiations, mainly during the disengagement talks with Egypt and ' . . . to make a supreme effort to strengthen the IDF by acquiring a maximum in arms . . . from the United States . . . and to take special measures in anti-terrorist campaign';[107] a not altogether surprising agenda given his past history. Domestically, he faced two problems: the rebuilding of the battered armed forces and averting the complete collapse of the economy. For the IDF he ordered a three-year rebuilding programme, a revision of its needs and the testing of the army's mobilisation procedures, and, most notably, a compilation of military aid required which he would present during his first visit to the United States as Prime Minister. Altogether he requested and was granted a military and economic aid package worth billions by the autumn of 1976.[108]

Economically, Israel suffered one of its worst periods since the state's establishment: as a result of the most recent war, inflation rose to 40 per cent and the trade deficit was increasing as steadily as consumer prices continued to rise. Rabin particularly lamented the 'booming black market' at the time and the growing gap between 'the "haves" and the "have nots"'.[109] His own preoccupation with defence and foreign affairs, to which he freely admitted in his autobiography, lead to him delegating 'the handling of these economic problems to Finance Minister Yehoshua Rabinovitch'.[110] Rabin and his Finance Minister called for an increase in exports while cutting imports, announced a 43 per cent devaluation of the Israeli pound, income tax reform and simultaneously introduced value added taxes. These measures were accompanied by government calls for necessary collective belt-tightening. Yet the public, faced with sharply-increased prices, was unconvinced and met these economic measures, as Rabin noted, 'with undisguised scorn'[111] and a series of strikes and, as in the case of the rather ill-named Tel Aviv slum quarter Hatikva (Hebrew for 'Hope'), even with riots. A popular joke at that time was one that played on the Hebrew word for 'bad', 'ra', and asked how to say bad, worse, worst, the correct answer was 'Ra, Rabin, Rabinovitch'.

Rabin was disappointed by the public's obstinacy. In October 1975 he appealed to his countrymen's reason when pleading that 'our economic future depends on every individual doing his job as unquestioningly as a soldier does'.[112] It was not the last time that Rabin had difficulties dealing with and comprehending the essential differences between commanding an army and leading a people. His strong sense of duty, and his respect and appreciation for a clear-cut chain of command where one man decided after careful consideration and the others followed without much ado, made it difficult for him to deal with the complexity of national as opposed to military

81

leadership. Never a very patient man, the need to explain his policies, and particularly the necessity of wining a disagreeing public over by careful reasoning, gruelling clarifications and repetitive explanations made for trying moments.

The first weeks of his premiership were considerably brightened by a 'political event unprecedented in Israel's history: the visit of an American president'. Nixon received a warm welcome in Israel, with Israelis lining the road from the airport near Tel Aviv to Jerusalem, and Rabin looking forward to hosting 'one of the most pro-Israeli presidents'.[113] But the American President was, in political terms, a dead man walking; the Watergate affair had irretrievably damaged his presidency and his days in office were numbered. Thus, when Rabin travelled to Washington in September, he was met by Nixon's successor, Gerald Ford. Rabin knew Ford from his tenure as ambassador and liked him. Yet, it was Ford who caused him shock and dismay. To Rabin's great horror the Americans had organised a ball after the state dinner. When the music began, Ford asked Leah to dance with him. Rabin did not know how to dance, 'not a step', but knew that it was expected of him now to ask Mrs Ford. Unsurprisingly she rose expectantly seeing Rabin making his way to her. But after 'swallowing hard' he carefully explained to her that, to his great regret, he would not be able to sweep her onto the dance floor since he was afraid of 'mauling'[114] her toes. Mrs Ford was unimpressed and countered that she used to teach dancing as a young woman. Fortunately, Henry Kissinger came to his rescue and Rabin remarked that if Kissinger 'had never done anything else for Israel, I would still be eternally grateful for that small mercy'.[115]

Politically, the visit centred on Rabin's request for additional American military and economic aid, discussions about the disengagement with Syria and Egypt and a future peace settlement. The near-defeat of 1973 not only caused the post-1967 sense of invincibility to give way to a profound sense of vulnerability and precariousness, but Israelis were also divided as to which conclusion the country had to draw from it. Whereas some argued that now, in a position of relative weakness, it was not the time to make concessions in order to attain some sort of peace, others claimed that the last war presented a 'window of opportunity' that should not be ignored. Rabin too believed that a peace agreement had to come about at some point. He believed that so far, all Arab–Israeli wars had been justified since the Arab states refused to recognise Israel's right to exist. War to him was not about winning the moral high ground but, like the Prussian general Karl von Clausewitz, whom he greatly admired and occasionally quoted, he believed that military force should only be used 'to achieve a political goal' and not be abused for a vain 'competition in operating airplanes and tanks'.[116] The outcome of the latest armed confrontation only reaffirmed his belief that Israel, despite its military superiority, would not be able to enforce its version of peace in its entirety on its neighbours and that a settlement of the conflict by non-violent means would eventually have to be negotiated. But, according to him – being the ever-so cautious and careful soldier – the time was not ripe for peace yet. In a conversation at that time with Shlomo Avineri, a political scholar at the Hebrew University and Director General of the Foreign Ministry, he explained that he knew that Israel could not hold on to the territories for ever and that a territorial exchange in return for peace was inevitable. But by no means, he continued, should Israel withdraw from the territories 'in the shadow of the Yom Kippur War . . . in a manner that looked as if it expressed Israeli weakness'.[117] Instead he wanted to concentrate on rebuilding the country militarily, economically and politically, which, as a result, would put Israel in a stronger negotiating position for peace talks in the future.

After the signing of the military disengagement agreement with Egypt and Syria, Rabin and his cabinet had to decide how they wanted to proceed. The cabinet was divided between what the next step should be; some favoured talks with Jordan, while others, among them Rabin, wanted to deal with Egypt first and work on an interim agreement. However, during the coming years Rabin met King Hussein over half a dozen times in secret meetings where the two of them discussed, among other things, how to reach a settlement, promote economic co-operation and to co-ordinate their policies towards Palestinian terrorist groups. But eventually it became clear that Rabin was not ready to offer Hussein a deal on the West Bank. He was probably too afraid of the domestic repercussions such a deal would have and he was very much aware how the generation of the founding fathers would react. King Hussein remembered his last meeting with Rabin in 1976. Rabin allegedly concluded it by saying that he, Hussein, should 'wait for ten years; maybe things will change on the ground'. It was a tactic 'to play for time, to postpone difficult decisions until the regional constellation had changed in Israel's favour, to survive politically'.[118]

With the Jordanian negotiations having reached a dead end Rabin turned his attention to Egypt. The agreement he eventually signed with Sadat was preceded by arduous shuttle diplomacy by Henry Kissinger. The American and Rabin had agreed that an overall peace settlement in the Middle East was out of reach and thus concentrated on an interim accord with

Egypt. Kissinger took it upon himself to oversee and mediate between both countries and frequently flew back and forth between Egypt to Israel to exchange proposals and ideas to bridge the gap between the two sides; often taking the liberty of deciding what exactly he would tell each side of the other's assessments. Rabin showed great stubbornness by insisting on receiving political rewards for every Israeli troop withdrawal from occupied Egyptian territory; he wanted a 'piece of peace' for every 'piece of land'.[119] What made Rabin's proposal so difficult for the Egyptians to accept was that he tried to take Egypt completely out of the conflict, a move Egypt could not afford politically. Even though Rabin and Kissinger held each other in high esteem, the American grew impatient with Rabin's intransigence and started to blame him for the deadlock. After yet another heated encounter with Kissinger in March 1975, Rabin received a letter from President Ford, expressing his disappointment in Rabin's obstinacy and said that, as a result, he would reassess his policy towards Israel. The following months, in which the Americans refused to sign any new arms deals, were one of the most difficult periods in the states' relations. Rabin, irritated, annoyed and convinced that the harsh note was Kissinger's idea not Ford's, was not impressed. On the contrary, now more than ever he believed that any agreement with Egypt should be entirely based on 'my perception of Israel's needs'.[120] In June Rabin flew to Washington to undo some of the harm that had been done. Ford confronted him with two options: Israel could finally work out an agreement with Egypt or he would give the go-ahead for an international conference at Geneva with the aim of an overall peace settlement. Rabin finally relented. The interim agreement was ratified on 3 September 1975 by the Knesset and formally signed a day later in Geneva. It did not bring peace but stated that the two countries would in future seek to solve their differences without the threat or use of force and work for a peace agreement; a demilitarised buffer zone came under the control of UN forces and zones where only limited numbers of troops were allowed were created. As a result Egypt reopened the Suez Canal which had been closed since 1967. But most decisive was the 'Memorandum of Understanding' between Israel and the United States. It promised a long-term American military and economic commitment to Israel. And it also entailed a separate, secret 'Memorandum of Agreement' in which the United States promised neither to recognise nor to talk with the PLO, who, to Rabin's great distress had recently scored several diplomatic victories: it was Rabin's way of making the Americans pay for his concessions to the Egyptians.

However, the biggest challenge Rabin faced and which showed his ambivalent policy with regards to a peace agreement, was an internal one: the growing Israeli settler movement.

The Enemy Within

The breeding ground in which Rabin's domestic challenger flourished was the contested territories, and the previous government's failure to develop a coherent policy concerning their future. Golda Meir had presided over a government that had consisted of no less than seven parties whose ideological and political backgrounds varied greatly. As a result it was unable to formulate a clear policy as to what to do with the new, and as the religious enthusiasts claimed, miraculously-gained, land. The ideologues claimed that the 'new' territories, especially the West Bank, were in fact none other than the ancient homeland of the Jews which was promised to them by God, and thus any territorial compromise would be nothing less than heresy. The pragmatists, on the other hand, were less concerned about biblical borders than about the viability of the state's newly-extended frontiers, their security implications and the political repercussions of holding on to land whose occupation the international community had deemed inconsistent with international law. In addition they were worried what would become of the Jewish State if it was to have to incorporate hundred of thousands of non-Jews.

In the end, Israel adopted the so-called Allon Plan. Yigal Allon, then Minister of Labour, had proposed that Israel should establish permanent defensive boundaries along the eastern borders of the West Bank but avoid settling near the heavily-populated Palestinian heartland, which, at some point, would be returned to Jordan in a peace settlement. Thus Israel embarked on its 'benevolent occupation', counting on the acquiescence of the Palestinians who it hoped would enjoy the economic benefits of Israeli rule and thus forget their national aspirations. Many Israeli politicians would later describe the late 1960s and early 1970s as a time of waiting for calls from Arab heads of state. They believed that the Arab states would eventually accept their military defeats and recognise that their lost territories could only be regained by negotiations, which would entail only the limited Israeli territorial withdrawals that the Labour Party advocated. However, there was a growing number of Jews who did not share any of the above-mentioned beliefs or fears but instead firmly believed that all of the West Bank should not only be retained but settled and thus physically reclaimed by the Jews. Soon after the end of the war the 'new' settlers, as opposed to the first settler generation, set up their makeshift homes on 'liberated land'. The Israeli government – which had immediately annexed East Jerusalem, to international protest, but had no intention of so doing with the West Bank and the Gaza Strip – viewed the religious settlers with concern. Yet, no serious effort was to stop them and gradually settlement after settlement was established which, eventually, received not only tacit government approval but also increased financial aid.

One of his first public encounters with the settlers, who for the most part belonged to the religious Gush Emunim ('Block of the Faithful') movement, was during one of Henry Kissinger's visits in Israel during his shuttle diplomacy. The American was greeted by 'an appalling display of anti-Semitism', with settlers calling him 'a Jew-boy' and 'the husband of a gentile women', they 'laid siege to the Knesset in an attempt to disrupt the reception' and voiced their protest at the American-brokered disengagement with Egypt that entailed the return of Sinai. Rabin was shocked and ashamed and wrote that he doubted that he 'shall ever witness more deplorable or misguided behaviour on the part of my countrymen'.[121] The differences between Rabin and the settlers were deep: Rabin had been raised in the spirit of national Zionism, where the Bible was turned into a document of national history, and at a time where every effort was made to secularise the Book of Books by supplementing religious holidays with national ones. He was not a religious man and was rarely seen in synagogues or wearing the traditional Jewish head covering, the Kippa. Religious texts to him were for personal consumption only, never the basis for political analysis. Thus he came to view the new settlers differently from the settler generation of his parents, not as righteous men but as people who seriously hindered a rational approach and political solution to the future of the territories. Thus, when in December 1975 he learned that thousands of Gush Emunim activists had congregated in an abandoned railway station in Sebastia, near the Palestinian city of Nablus in the West Bank, with the intention of establishing a settlement, he at once ordered their removal.

He sent, among others, Ariel Sharon, to talk the would-be settlers into leaving – a poor choice considering the fact that the hawkish Sharon had joined several sit-ins with settlers in the past. But his true opponent turned out to be Shimon Peres. When Sharon reported back to Rabin, he told him that Peres, who at that time was leaning much more to the political right than Rabin and who was in fact their main government contact and political sponsor,[122] had already offered them a deal. Rabin, once more put out by the independent actions of his rival, turned to Mordechai Gur, then Chief of Staff. He asked him whether it was possible to remove the would-be settlers, as had been done before, by limited force and without triggering violence and how many soldiers would be needed. Gur told him that he would need about a brigade, 3,000 men. However, he strongly argued against such a move fearing that, given the number of soldiers and the unpredictability of the situation, an enforced eviction might turn violent. At one point he even threatened to resign if Rabin gave the go-ahead despite his reservations. But Rabin yielded, like Gur fearing a clash between the soldiers and the settlers. In the end he was neither strong enough to stand the pressure nor able to see the long-lasting impact his backing-off would have. Despite his better judgement he allowed, as a 'temporary measure', 30 settler families to move into a nearby IDF base close to the village of Kaddum, a few miles from Nablus. Rabin never attempted to remove them. He later justified his inaction and failure of leadership as the result of his rivalry with Shimon Peres, who, with his hawkish views and personal resentment, enforced the Kaddum arrangement on him. But this ill-fated compromise – which resulted in a 45 per cent increase in settlement activity between mid-1975 and 1977[123] – set the pattern for his future relationship with the settlers.

It was marked by contempt, a dangerous lack of understanding of their ferocity and his wish to, if not to avoid, then at least to postpone any confrontation which would ultimately test his political will as much as his leadership skills. Even when he became Prime Minister for the second time, his contradictory position towards the settlers, his disrespect and loathing for them on the one hand, his submission and carelessness on the other, eventually led him to ignore the impact they had on his policies and their growing radicalisation. It would cost him dearly and not only in political terms.

It was not only internal political rivalry and ideological clashes that marked his first premiership: there were also moments of high drama. It was on Sunday 27 June 1976 that Rabin was informed that Air France Flight 139 from Tel Aviv to Paris had been hijacked after a brief stopover in Athens. Among the 230 passengers were 83 Israelis. By Monday, the plane had landed in Entebbe, Uganda and the hijackers, a mixed group of Arabs and Germans, set out their demands: the release of 53 of their 'freedom fighters' who were held in various countries, 40 of them in Israeli prisons, in return for the hostages. Rabin instantly formed a special ministerial team including among others Shimon Peres, and set out a double strategy. On the one hand he declared Israel's willingness to release prisoners as part of a negotiated deal under the auspices of the French government – the plane fell under France's jurisdiction – while on the other hand he asked the IDF to prepare a military option. Under great pressure several strategies were developed, among them a 'truly bizarre proposal . . . with the backing of the defence minister . . . for Moshe Dayan to go and talk with Idi Amin . . . Uganda's unpredictable tyrant', which was discarded before Rabin decided on the 'Hercules Plan', the only 'plan I could consider as reasonably feasible'[124] which involved an Israeli assault involving Hercules transport aircraft. After a successful dry run on 2 July, close to the hijacker's deadline, Rabin sent the planes on their way without prior cabinet approval. The cabinet was supposed to meet on in the early afternoon of 3 July, but Rabin could not wait any longer and if need be, would have rather recalled the planes than possibly jeopardise the operation by any further delay. But the cabinet approved and Rabin, having experienced the full burden of decision-making, went home 'feeling calm for the first time in a week'.[125] Operation Hercules was a complete success with only four Israelis killed, three hostages and the commander of the force, Jonathan Netanjahu. Rabin admitted that 'considering the circumstances in which the assault was carried out' – the most spectacular IDF operation carried out outside Israeli territory – 'the number of casualties was smaller than I had dared to hope'.[126]

But success, unlike failure, has many fathers, and Rabin was not surprised that Peres tried to gain political capital out of the event, basing his claim for praise on the fact that it was actually he who has suggested a military operation and not Rabin. Rabin, of course, would remember things differently and recalled that Peres in fact never even consulted the Chief of Staff about rescuing the hostages. Be that as it may, for Rabin it was just further proof that his political rivals, that is Peres and his supporters, stopped short of nothing to 'undermine my standing and advance their own ambitions'.[127]

Entebbe also boosted Israel's popularity around the world which had reached a significant low in the last year. The reasons were twofold: the joint declaration of the Arab states during a summit at Rabat in October 1974 that the PLO was the sole representative of the Palestinians and that they, as a people, had the right to establish a national authority in any

Palestinian territory that was liberated, thus stripping King Hussein of any role in an eventual settlement of the Palestinian question and giving weight to the Palestinians' claim that only they were able and responsible to negotiate about their collective future. This was followed by a speech by Yassir Arafat to the United Nations General Assembly a month later. In it Arafat emphasised the legitimacy of armed resistance in light of the illegal occupation of Palestinian territory and called for Palestinian self-determination and the creation of a secular democratic state in what was Israel. Arafat's speech won the Palestinians and their cause unprecedented international recognition. A year later Israel suffered another blow when the UN Assembly called the Jewish State a racist regime that 'occupied Palestine' with its underlying ideology, Zionism, being nothing else but 'a form of . . . racial discrimination'. The success at Entebbe won Israel badly-needed international sympathy. Rabin's popularity surged to unprecedented levels as a result; it seemed that it was no longer a question of whether Labour and Rabin would win the upcoming elections, but how big their victory would be. But the following months, marred by political intrigues, scandal and personal misfortune, saw the end of his premiership.

Rabin might have been a new face in politics, but the party he headed was not. As the new Governor of the Bank of Israel, he had chosen Asher Yadlin, a long-time Labour party member and former head of the Histadrut trade union's health organisation which, since its beginning, had been dominated by the Labour Party. Shortly after Yadlin's nomination rumours began to circulate that he was under police investigation concerning accusations of corruption. Rabin withdrew his candidate but to the majority of Israelis it was an untimely reminder that the party under Rabin was still the party of Golda Meir. In addition, Rabin's Housing Minister and friend, Avraham Ofer, first came in for criticism and then under investigation regarding claims that he had misused party funds. Ofer was still being investigated when he took his own life on 3 January 1977, a few months before the elections. Rabin was dismayed and upset by the press coverage of the case which he believed had 'massacred him' before even a 'shred of evidence was found'. He was convinced that 'the trigger of his gun had been pulled by an intemperate public and a press that permitted itself to condemn a man before he was even accused of a crime'.[128] Moreover, Rabin's government, carefully held together for the past few years, had fallen apart. The reason was a ceremony for the delivery of the first American F-15 fighters that had taken place on a Saturday, the Jewish day of rest and thus, in the eyes of his religious coalition partners, had unnecessarily violated the holy day. As a protest the National Religious Party (NRP) refused to support Rabin in a no-confidence vote. Rabin, tired of haggling with them, dismissed the NRP ministers and his government became a caretaker one. The new elections were brought forward to mid-May which encouraged Peres to challenge Rabin's candidacy. The result was a fierce and ugly contest that Rabin only narrowly won by 41 votes in February 1977. But squabbles between Rabin and Peres continued to dominate the headlines and the Labour Party presented anything but a united front. They openly argued about the necessity or futility of settlements, over the defence budget and their positions in the party. Rabin even accused Peres of undermining his authority by leaking classified government information. However, what eventually would cause the abrupt and rather dishonourable end of his first premiership was of his own making.

In 1976, Rabin went to Washington for a first visit with Jimmy Carter, the new President,. While Rabin discovered that the new American President was much less inclined to support Israel unreservedly, particularly because of Israel's refusal to consider even talking with the Palestinians, Leah took advantage of a small gap in her schedule and went to the Dupont Circle branch of the National Bank where she and her husband had jointly held two accounts since his time as ambassador. Leah withdrew the remaining $2,000 and closed the accounts. It was a small sum and there was nothing illicit about the accounts apart from the fact that they were, according to Israel's stringent currency regulations, illegal; no Israeli citizen was allowed to hold a foreign bank account unless they were living abroad.

Upon Rabin's return to Israel he heard from his media advisor Dan Pattir that he had just received a telephone call from a journalist of the Israeli daily newspaper *Ha'aretz*. Dan Margalit, the paper's Washington correspondent, had learned by chance of the Rabins' accounts and now wanted to know, after having verified their existence by depositing $50 in them, whether Pattir knew that the Israeli Prime Minister had violated the laws of his country. Rabin at first refused to react. After the article's publication, which caused no public outcry, with most Israelis willing to give Rabin the benefit of the doubt, the Attorney General nevertheless began an investigation. Even though Rabin frequently referred to Leah as the family's 'finance minister', there was no question that they 'morally and formally shared responsibility equally'.[129] He did what he thought was the honourable thing: he withdrew his candidacy on 7 April 1977.

It was particularly ironic that Leah should have been the cause of this unlucky ending. She was not only the one who took care of the family so Rabin could concentrate on his career; she was also his greatest supporter. According to a close friend and aide, she supported his position as army commander and believed in his potential. She actively rallied support for him by organising lunch and dinner parties to which everyone who could advance his political career was invited, in order to place him in the post she thought he deserved: the Israeli premiership.

Rabin's resignation, a decision infused with a soldier's sense of honour, was an unprecedented occurrence in Israeli public and particularly political life. Many personal and political friends tried to persuade him not to quit but he dismissed them, insisting that a 'man is truly alone at such times'[130] and that no one would be able to change his mind. Instead he took leave of absence and went on vacation with Leah. She stood trial on 17 April and was faced with the choice between paying a fine of 250,000 Israeli Pounds or a year in prison. Needless to say they paid the fine.

Rabin's successor was none other than Shimon Peres who took over Labour's election campaign. Rabin himself avoided the public as much as he could, refused to give interviews and kept out of the limelight. Israel went to vote on 17 May. Polls had predicted yet another Labour victory but a large number of undecided voters had made it difficult to foretell the exact result. The country was in for a big surprise: Israelis, thoroughly fed up and disillusioned with their Labour governments, disturbed by the strained relationship with America and disappointed that peace was just as far away as ever, voted for the first time and overwhelmingly for the opposition, the right-wing Likud. Likud, however, had also managed to attract many voters of African and Asian backgrounds, the Mizrahi, who felt excluded from the mostly European born and bred leadership, the Ashkenasim. Many of them had come to Israel in the 1950s and felt, upon their arrival, alienated from their new countrymen. The Mizrahi Jews were generally more traditional, more religious and had lived for most of their lives under repressive regimes. Many of them still wore side-locks and traditional clothes which were often laughed at by the Sabras, the native secularised and worldly Jews. The Mizrahi had complained for a long time of feeling looked down on, of having been shunted to development towns where Israeli Jews did not wish to live and doing manual labour the Sabras did not want to do and they bitterly resented 'the fact that Labour leaders often responded to their complaints by calling them culturally inferior'. Ben Gurion once even remarked about Moroccan Jews 'that their costumes are those of Arabs. They love their women, but beat them . . . Maybe in the third generation something will appear from the Oriental Jew that is different. But I don't see it yet'.[131] Particularly during economic crises, when shortages of jobs and housing became more obvious, Mizrahi Jews occasionally clashed violently with the police. It happened in 1959 in the Wadi Salib, a formerly Palestinian neighbourhood in Haifa, where a minor incident between a policeman and a worker of Mizrahi origin exposed the gap between rich and poor, and led to unrest. The newly-formed Likud, under the leadership of Menachem Begin, was able to exploit these sentiments and grievances and managed to turn the Likud party – the result of a merger in 1973 between Menachem Begin's Herut, formerly the Irgun, and Gahal, a liberal party and several smaller parties from the right – into a party for the excluded, the underdogs and a true alternative for the Labour party that had controlled the country for so long.

Thus, after 29 years in government, the Labour Party had to submit to the role of opposition and Yitzhak Rabin went with it, going from Prime Minister to Knesset backbencher in less than two months.

One Among Many:
The Opposition Years, 1977–1984

Rabin handed over his office to the new Prime Minister Menachem Begin on 21 June 1977. He was sure that Labour's defeat was the price the party had to pay 'for the intrigues, conflicts and internal dissension that had divided its ranks'[132] in the run-up to the election and thus put the blame squarely on Peres. He felt his office was unfairly taken from him not least by Peres whom with contempt and barely-concealed wrath he called 'an inveterate schemer'. Dan Pattir once said that Rabin 'believed that he was a victim of the tricks of the game. I didn't hear him blame Peres directly but he felt there had been an effort within the Labour Party to push him out'.[133] Peres, of course, saw things differently and never, at least not retrospectively, recalled 'any animosity from him, nor did I harbour any towards him'. He would only admit that due to their different political backgrounds there was 'not . . . a special comradeship between us', yet, all in all their relationship 'was wholesome and proper . . . until we ran against each other'.[134]

But there was at least one advantage of being an opposition Knesset member: spare time. In spring 1977 Dalia gave birth to her second child, a girl called Noa. Noa and her brother Jonathan, three years her senior, came to spend a considerable amount of time with their grandparents after Dalia's marriage ran into trouble. As curt as he could be with people who did not match his idea of competence and intelligence, Rabin was very patient and committed to his grandchildren. When Jonathan, still a toddler, refused to eat, Rabin would turn a spoonful of food into some imaginary 'AMX-13 or Patton tank', move it through the air and eventually thrust it into Jonathan's mouth thus coaxing him patiently into eating. He taught his granddaughter at a very early age to play chess, meticulously explaining to her every move and strategy. His daughter recalled that she was surprised at her children's lack of inhibition and the easiness with which they would bother him with any 'nonsense they could think of', something neither she nor her brother would have dared to do when they had been children.[135] This close relationship lasted well into their teenage years and their grandfather always tried to find time for them even after his schedule got considerably busier again.

But as much as he enjoyed the time he was able to spend with his family, in foreign travel and with a much better work–life balance, he was bored and frustrated. He came to view his time at the top as a period of personal failure; he knew that he had failed to reign in his rivals and to assert his authority over the party and his government. Furthermore, his prudent politics of wait-and-see and his guarded, uncreative approach to the Arab–Israeli conflict had brought peace no nearer. His political future must also have looked somewhat bleak to him. He still had supporters in the Labour party, but generally the party was firmly controlled by Peres and any return to national leadership or even a greater political role would have to take place under his arch rival, a rather unpleasant prospect.

While Rabin slowly settled into his new life, Israel underwent a thorough transformation. Menachem Begin led a party that was ideologically deeply committed to the 'integrity of the homeland' to which it believed the Jews had an eternal right, adhering to a manifesto that claimed 'between the sea and the Jordan, there will be Jewish sovereignty alone'[136] and which never even entertained the idea of anything that might resemble a Palestinian state. Consistent with its ideological commitment, the new government actively encouraged and intensified the settlement of the territories. Likud deliberately set out to transform and create a new reality, the position on the ground, which would render any return of the territories impossible: 'we do not even dream of the possibility – if we are given the chance to withdraw our military forces from Judea, Samaria and Gaza – of abandoning these areas to the control of the murderous organisation that is called the PLO . . . we have a right and a demand for [Israel] sovereignty over these areas of Eretz Israel. This is our land and it belongs to the Jewish nation rightfully',[137] as Begin said in a speech to the Knesset in December 1977.

But not only the parties differed: Menachem Begin was also the complete opposite of the sabra Rabin. Born in Russia in 1913 in a small town where the Zionist movement was very active, at an early age he became a member of the ultranationalist and authoritarian Betar Youth movement founded by Ze'ev Jabotinsky, an ardent Jewish nationalist. Jabotinsky was an exceptional orator, political thinker and militant defender of the Jews' right to settle on both banks of the Jordan. He had always rejected mainstream Zionism and its 'unrealistic' ideas of

101

any non-military solution to Arab resistance to the Jewish state and as a result, founded the Revisionist movement. He had lamented the 'first partition' of Palestine in 1922 and was convinced that the Arabs will only consent to a Jewish state when kept at bay with an 'Iron Wall' of Jewish military power. The other seminal influence on Begin was the experience of the Holocaust. He lost his parents and brother to Nazi savagery and this ordeal not only haunted him personally for the rest of his life, but became the ultimate prism and framework through which he perceived and conducted Israel's relations with the non-Jewish world; a world, he was sure, that was unremittingly anti-Semitic, by and large hostile and consequently not to be trusted.

Begin's election was viewed with apprehension by the international community thanks to his reputation as a warmonger and hawk; and he began his premiership with a speech that reinforced their fears. He reiterated the Jews' eternal and historic right to the whole of the land and said that he would start building settlements on a large scale on the land that was the inheritance of the Jews' forefathers. Yet, he continued with the pledge that his government would actively try to reach a peace agreement with Israel's neighbours. The Arabs were not impressed, particularly since Begin's intentions to encourage further Jewish settlements in the territories ran counter to their demands for the land to be returned.

Begin also went straight onto a collision course with Jimmy Carter. Rabin had already had a glimpse of the gulf that separated Israel's position from that of the President, but Begin's ideological stance made it only wider. What particularly irked the Israelis, among them Rabin, was the attention Carter paid to the Palestinians. From the beginning Israel had done everything to keep them outside of a conflict it perceived as being one solely between itself and the Arab states; a solution of the Palestinian problem was supposed to be a by-product of an overall peace agreement. When Rabin was in Washington for the last time as Prime Minister, he had to fend off questions from his American hosts, who asked him why Israel consistently refused to talk with the Palestinians when even the United States had managed to meet with the Vietcong. Rabin had answered with a question of his own, and inquiring whether the Vietcong had ever refused 'to recognise the existence of the States' and called 'for its annihilation?';[138] for him, as for most Israelis, that was the end of the discussion. But this historically-arguable comparison did not help Begin, who was faced with an American President saying out loud the unspeakable: the need for a 'Palestinian homeland'. Carter also insisted on Israeli territorial concessions and the acceptance of the PLO, which Begin had called a 'Nazi-Organisation' during the election campaign. The only concession Begin felt able to make was in regard to Egypt; basically taking the interim agreement Rabin had brokered one step further. Various international developments and the irreconcilability of the positions of the parties in question made Carter realise that he would not be able to achieve an overall settlement. Instead, he wanted to concentrate on an Israeli–Egyptian peace accord.

The initiative was finally taken by Anwar Sadat on 9 December 1977. In an address to an astounded Egyptian National Assembly he declared that he was willing to go to Jerusalem if that was what it took to achieve peace. Rabin, who once said that he believed that the 'key to the future relations between the Arab states and Israel lies in Israel's relationship with Egypt' because it was Egypt that had 'led the Arab countries into every war with Israel; it was always the first country to halt the fighting by agreeing to a cease-fire; and it has always been the first of the Arab countries to conclude agreements with Israel',[139] heard the announcement in Washington. He at once went to the American Secretary of State, Cyrus Vance, and asked whether he believed that Sadat was serious and would indeed come to Israel. Vance thought that the chances were fifty-fifty. Rabin, still stunned, returned to Israel and arrived only a day before the plane that brought an Arab leader to Israel for the first time touched down. The next day he found himself 'on the receiving line waiting' and was 'possessed by a strange feeling'. Egypt was, after all, 'the enemy'. When he saw Sadat appearing in the doorway of his plane 'our emotions peaked in a way I hadn't thought possible' and he 'felt like he was caught up in a dream'.[140]

Sadat spoke before the Knesset and gave a well-received speech which, in its carefulness, made it easy for the Israelis to agree to. Even though Sadat claimed that he understood Israel's need for security but not for land – 'an inherent contradiction'[141] according to Rabin – he appeased the Israelis by not mentioning the PLO, let alone persisting with the idea that Israel should enter talks with it. But the historic visit was followed by a political stalemate: while Sadat was adamant that an Egyptian–Israeli agreement should contain references to Israeli recognition of the Palestinian right to self-determination, Begin tried to include a guarantee for Israel's continuing hold on the West Bank. In addition, the Egyptians were annoyed by Begin's frequent mentioning of the Palestinians in the context of Nazism, and thus, as the Egyptians saw it, by inference other Arabs as well. Other contested issues were the extent of Israeli withdrawal, the use of Egyptian oil fields, Israeli settlements and Begin's refusal to adhere to UN Resolution 242. In the end the Americans called a summit to resolve the matter. The Camp David talks took place from 5–17 September 1978 and an agreement was reached after days of onerous and exhausting negotiations. After the Knesset's approval, with Rabin voting in favour, the Camp David Accords were signed in Washington in March 1979. The two sides had agreed to the establishment of peaceful relations between Israel and Egypt, an Israeli pullback from Sinai and a clause referring to Palestinian autonomy and 'the legitimate rights of the Palestinian people'. Begin had accepted the passage since, in its elusiveness, it left Israel with enough leverage and room for interpretation. Not surprisingly the subsequent negotiations concerning Palestinian autonomy did not bear any fruit.

Rabin, at Begin's invitation, was present during the signing ceremony; 'a recognition of my contribution in paving the way for the final peace process'.[142] He was satisfied with the step-by-step approach contained in the Camp David accords and believed it to be the proper starting-point for the countries to work for the 'invaluable goal of starting to build confidence, eliminating suspicion, hatred, and a misunderstanding of each other's problems'.[143] The indistinct reference to the Palestinians was apt, too; he neither believed nor did he 'accept that the notion of autonomy' was the right 'basis for the ultimate solution' to the, admittedly, 'thorniest problems we will have to face in the coming years'.[144] Even though he acknowledged the 'terrible human tragedy' that had taken place in 1947–8 he was sure that it was entirely 'created by the Arab countries'[145] when they rejected the UN partition of 1947.

He was not ready, and would in fact never be, to admit any Israeli wrongdoing. His approach to the Palestinian problem was based solely on security considerations. In the years to come he would change his assessment as to how to solve the problem but he never went as far as accepting any moral responsibility in the name of Israel nor would he accept genuine

Palestinian rights: as a soldier he was never trained in aspects of morality and justice. And as an Israeli raised on the rightfulness of the Zionist claim he was not able to concede to other people the same rights he claimed for his own. Only what he perceived as Israel's security needs mattered in the end.

When a year later Begin asserted Israel's right to the whole of Jerusalem by declaring it the official capital of the Jewish state, Rabin tried to reclaim the leadership of the Labour Party. A couple of months previously he had published his memoirs to explain but mainly to justify his actions as Prime Minister, and to vent his anger at Peres. He hoped that his book might discredit and sufficiently damage Peres' reputation so that he, Rabin, could take centre-stage again as the party's chief candidate during the June 1981 elections. The continuous bad blood between the two made it difficult for Peres to present a united front to the Israeli public. Rabin had openly backed Yigal Allon as the new party leader and had been indifferent to Peres' pleas to maintain party discipline. In a television interview in 1979 he vindicated his actions by saying that 'three years ago, those who so loudly proclaimed the virtues of competition for the party leadership, although there was a Labour prime minister at the time, are precisely those who say that this is unacceptable'.[146] Many party friends had urged Rabin not to publish the book, afraid that the revelations would severely reduce Labour's election chances. But Rabin's mind was set: Peres would pay. Peres was angry and countered Rabin's accusation by saying that 'his charges are very general in nature, and reflect more his problems than mine. The book will cause great harm to its author . . . and we will have to take the damage which Rabin did to the party into account'.[147] And indeed, Rabin's revenge boomeranged: not only did the party

106

members refuse to rebel against Peres, they turned their venom against Rabin. The Labour Party Secretariat called a meeting in which party members – among them many of Rabin's former ministers – wanted to pass a resolution condemning the book. But Peres eventually stopped the move, afraid that it would only widen the already deep rift; a decision many claimed that was actually playing into Rabin's hands because Peres' 'weak response' led many to accept Rabin's 'version of events . . . and the accusations against Peres took root'.[148] Rabin, undeterred, furious and without thinking about the possible negative consequences for the party, openly turned up the heat in several interviews about the public feud and said repeatedly that he stood by every word and that if anyone wanted to sue him they could. To those party members who wanted to punish him politically he replied 'I have no intention of abandoning political life' and reaffirming his claim to the party: 'I joined the movement at a very young age before I even heard of Shimon Peres . . . hence my membership in the party is not contingent on any particular man at its helm'.[149] His anger at Peres resulted in a high-handedness that made him not only unable to understand that it takes always two to tango but also oblivious to the damage the Labour Party suffered due to his mud-slinging and personal vendetta. When, in February 1980, Yigal Allon suddenly died, he was ready to run against Peres once more and by October he declared that he would run for Prime Minister if chosen by the party. His decision seemed justified since polls predicted not only a likely Labour win but also showed that Rabin was more popular than Begin and Peres: the public obviously preferred the straightforward and curt ex-soldier, ex-ambassador and ex-prime minister over the party animal whose reputation as an untrustworthy schemer it had absorbed. But the public was not the party and in December the Labour Party cast a clear vote for Peres.

Despite the predicted election victory, Labour's lead over Likud reduced continuously as the Likud campaigners, as a welcome and unexpected gift, quoted extensively from Rabin's book to undermine Peres' credibility and leadership qualities. Several party members urged Rabin to forbid the Likud to do this or at least to take the edge off of some of the things he had said and written. But their pleas fell on deaf ears: Rabin did no such thing and even carefully avoided, while campaigning in his usual tongue-tied and awkward manner, mentioning Peres' name.

Aside from Labour's self-destructive infighting, Begin managed to turn things around by attacking and destroying Iraq's nuclear reactor, which was believed to be the basis for a nuclear weapons programme and seen as a threat to Israel. The attack was internationally condemned but well-received by the Israeli public which liked this show of strength and unilateral decision; it boosted Begin's popularity and opinion polls started to predict a Likud victory. Peres, alarmed by the results, consulted with Rabin and asked him to serve as Defence Minister under his leadership and thus increase Labour's chances of winning. To everyone's surprise, Rabin agreed, even though in the summer he had proclaimed that he would never serve under Peres. This surprise move came too late: Likud won with one seat more than Labour and the truce between the Rabin and Peres soon faltered. But Begin's second term did not last long; he resigned after only two years. The reason for his departure and subsequent life as a recluse was the consequences of his ill-advised invasion of Israel's neighbour, Lebanon.

The small state north of Israel was a country riven with religious and political tension. It was a weak state from the outset and consequently easy prey to outside interference, and from the mid-1970s it was crippled by a civil war in which the PLO played a critical role. After its defeat and consequent ejection from Jordan, Lebanon had become the new base of the PLO, where a substantial number of Palestinians lived in refugee camps and from which it launched attacks against Israel. The embattled Christian Maronites, to whom Israel felt some affiliation due to their shared minority status, their opposition to Arab hegemony and their fight against the PLO, had appealed for help from its southern neighbour and Syria. In Israel many saw this as an opportunity to establish a friendly regime in Lebanon which, as a result, would make peace. Rabin, then Prime Minister, was sceptical and afraid that Israel would be dragged unnecessarily into a sticky situation. He wanted to keep Lebanon as a buffer between Israel and Syria and was against active Israeli involvement. Instead, he opted to help the Christians to help themselves and agreed to sub-stantial arms deliveries and assistance to Christian militias in the south of Lebanon. In addition Rabin accepted intervention by the Syrians, who claimed they wanted to restore order and to disarm the increasingly-active PLO fighters. But while tacitly agreeing to the Syrian presence, Rabin had established certain 'red lines' with regards to Syria which would keep both countries out of each other's way. The 'deterrent umbrella' Israel set up in the south of Lebanon, however, enabled the PLO to find shelter there: the Maronites were unable to disarm them and the 'red lines' stopped the Syrians from doing so. Israel tried to change this when it invaded Lebanon in 1982.

The main architect of the invasion was Ariel Sharon, Begin's Defence Minister. His ultimate aim was Israeli political hege-mony in the Middle East which he sought to achieve by first destroying the PLO and secondly by establishing a Maronite government in Lebanon. Sharon wanted not only a limited attack on PLO positions but envisioned the complete destruction of the PLO infrastructure and leadership in Lebanon. Sharon's wish went hand-in-hand with the tightening of Israel's occupation in the West Bank, where Palestinian land continued to be confiscated by the Israeli state, where Palestinian affairs were run by military administrators and where Israel actively tried to curtail any expression of Palestinian nationalism. Sharon hoped that by destroying the PLO leadership he would bring an end to Palestinian nationalism altogether. In addition he planned to drive out the Syrians and establish a Maronite regime. Since Sharon's plan found no support in the cabinet, he adopted different tactics, showing the ministers only part of his plan and keeping the rest to himself, knowing that once war broke out, there were few who could stop him from doing what he really wanted. Begin, of whom it is not known whether he was informed of Sharon's overall plan or only given the same incomplete information as the rest of the political establishment – and of course, the public – sent emissaries to Washington to inform the Americans about Israel's plan for a limited attack. However, the new president, Ronald Reagan, insisted that Israel was only to attack when provoked. An attempt on the life of Israel's ambassador in London, carried out by a rival group to Arafat's PLO, was all it took for Israel to attack PLO positions in West Beirut. When the PLO shelled the north of Israel in retaliation, the cabinet approved what it believed was only a limited invasion of Lebanon on 6 June 1982.

Rabin initially supported the war, in particular Sharon's attempt to destroy PLO bases. When Israeli troops advanced to Beirut and laid siege to the city, he not only sanctioned it but recommended Sharon tighten the cordon and to continue the disruption of water and electricity supplies to the civilian population. When the IDF heavily bombarded the city he said 'I can live with a twenty-four hour bombardment of Beirut'.[150] Some attributed his hawkishness during the initial stage in the war as an expression of support for the IDF in line with his belief in *macht politik* and, since the military machine was in action, it should be allowed to make the most of it. One of the pictures that contributed most to his growing image as a militant hawk was of him and Sharon watching the siege of Beirut, both clad in flak jackets. Only later, when the swift and effective stroll into Lebanon turned into a quagmire, and Sharon set out to achieve his other objectives, did Rabin start to speak out against the war. The Lebanese leader Sharon had envisioned making peace with Israel, Bashir Gemayel, was assassinated and thus the main pillar of his strategy collapsed. However, worse was to come. Between 16 and 18 September 1982, Christian militiamen, in plain view of the Israeli forces and with their tactic consent, murdered at least 800 and perhaps as many as 2,000 Palestinians, including many women and children and not, as claimed, PLO fighters, in the Sabra and Shatila refugee camps on the outskirts of Beirut. In the aftermath of the slaughter Israel tried to hide the fact that the militia had entered the refugee camps with IDF approval, but international and widespread domestic revulsion led to the establishment of the Kahane Commission which found Ariel Sharon and Chief of Staff Rafael Eitan indirectly responsible for it.

The Lebanese war was a complete failure: it undermined Israel's international standing, led to its partial withdrawal and subsequent Syrian control of Lebanon and did not bring peace to Israel's north as promised. Domestically the war destroyed the IDF's myth of 'purity of arms', the widely-held

111

belief that the Jewish army only fought to defend, not to attack. Numerous peace groups sprang up, all expressing their anger at Sharon and this ill-advised war. In short, for many Israelis, including some of its soldiers, their state had lost its innocence. Rabin drew the conclusion from it that 'there is a fundamental error in the approach that uses military might to achieve the total imposition of our political will over an Arab state or a group of Arab states'.[151] But this lesson did not change his attitude towards the PLO. The only one who accepted responsibility was Menachem Begin. While Sharon did not recognise the findings of the commission and only grudgingly gave up his Defence Ministry job, Begin announced his resignation on 28 August 1983. The only reason he gave was that he 'could not go on' and he spent the rest of his life as a recluse. Even though he never explained his decision in detail – the death of his wife the previous year probably having added to his weariness – it is fair to assume the war he said would last only two days but showed no sign of ending and the deaths of hundreds of soldiers, contributed to it.

Begin's successor was Yitzhak Shamir who in the year before the next election was forced to deal with the legacy of the invasion and a crippling economic crisis in which inflation reached 400 per cent. The ideological hawk's dull and uninspiring personality did not fare particularly well with the Israeli electorate and on 23 July 1984 Likud had three seats less than its political opponents. Neither Peres nor Shamir were able to attract enough coalition partners, and both parties were forced into a government of national unity. The new Prime Minister was Shimon Peres who was to be replaced by Shamir after two years in office. And the new Minister of Defence chosen to serve the full four years was Yitzhak Rabin.

Minister of Defence: 1984–1989

Shortly before the election the question of the party leadership had come up once more. This time the contenders were not only Peres and Rabin but another candidate: Yitzhak Navon. After careful consideration Rabin had concluded that it would not only be in the interest of the party, but also to his own benefit if he ever wanted to play a more influential role, to support Peres. A secret meeting between Peres and Rabin was arranged and after a slightly awkward start, Rabin expressed his confidence in Peres and, in return, asked for his support in his bid to become Defence Minister. It was a request Peres felt able to agree to. As a result, Navon bowed out and Peres was Labour's undisputed candidate.

The new government was sworn in on 14 September 1984 and Leah remembered Yitzhak's return to government as a homecoming of sorts after years on the political sidelines. Shimon Peres was in the eyes of many political commentators a surprisingly successful Prime Minister. He was well prepared and immediately started to tackle Israel's economic problems.

He also initiated the IDF's withdrawal from Lebanon despite the Likud's opposition and with the help of Yitzhak Rabin. All Israel held on to was a self-declared security zone in the south. Rabin justified the withdrawal by explaining that he had neither the intention nor was it in Israel's interests to police the area for ever: the Israeli public could not have agreed more.

The period also witnessed an array of efforts at negotiations to reach peace between Israel and its neighbours. Peres tried his best to salvage some of the reputation Israel had forfeited so carelessly during the invasion of Lebanon and attempted to strike a separate deal with Jordan concerning the Palestinians without having to deal with the PLO which, as a result of the latest confrontation, had sought refuge in Tunis. The Israeli government and its Defence Minister stuck to the conviction that, even if the PLO would accept UN Resolutions 242 and 338 – the successor and confirmation of the validity of Resolution 242 and in place since the 1973 war – even talking with it would equal Israeli willingness to consent to a Palestinian state in the future. Peres continued his negotiations with Jordan despite opposition from the Likud. Rabin was sent to meet with King Hussein several times in secret where they continued the talks that had reached a dead end during his premiership. As Defence Minister the occupied territories fell under his responsibility and he complained to King Hussein about the increase in Palestinian attacks, demanding that he put an end to them. In exchange for strengthening economic ties between the two countries, Hussein complied and ordered the closure of the remaining PLO office in Amman. When Shamir became Prime Minister, with Peres taking over the Foreign Ministry, he tried his best to sabotage any efforts to reach an agreement. Shamir, who wholeheartedly believed his own statement that 'the Arabs are the same Arabs and the sea is the same sea', thought that peace should be given to Israel without any concessions. Thus when Peres reached an agreement with King Hussein to set up an international conference to solve the conflict on the basis of the UN resolutions 'with the object of bringing a comprehensive peace to the area, security to its states, and to respond to the legitimate rights of the Palestinian people',[152] Shamir did everything possible to cripple it. Nevertheless the events of the following months made it quite clear that the Palestinian problem could not be ignored anymore: the Palestinians launched their first popular mass resistance against Israeli occupation, a development many observers of Israeli politics had long seen coming and which the Lebanon war had made clearer as two Israeli journalists noted in 1984 in the afterword of their book *Israel's Lebanon War*: 'the war . . . has in no way tempered the virulence of the Palestinian problem – which is hardly surprising, inasmuch as the roots of that problem do not lie in Lebanon. It was sheer folly to believe that any action there would ameliorate the political conflict between the Israeli and Palestinian nations'.[153] How right they were was proved in the last month of 1987.

Throwing Stones and Breaking Bones

The 'Intifada', Arabic for 'shaking off', started in December 1987 in the Jebalya refugee camp in the Gaza Strip. It was preceded by an incident in which an Israeli truck crashed into a group of Palestinians, killing four of them and injuring several others. During the funerals, demonstrations erupted that quickly spread to the West Bank. It was a spontaneous expression of anger and pent-up disappointment directed at the Israelis but also a sign of frustration with the failure of the external

115

Palestinian leadership and other Arab states to pay adequate attention to the dire situation of the Palestinians in the territories.

And indeed, Israeli rule in the occupied territories was harsh: Palestinian land was regularly confiscated, the press and schoolbooks were censored, national leaders were often deported and collective punishments like curfews and house demolitions were frequently used to suppress any expression of Palestinian nationalism. With fear the Palestinians watched the unabated Israeli settlement drive and the expansion of Jewish Jerusalem into Palestinian areas.

When Yitzhak Rabin learned of the spreading demonstrations he saw no need to act; he was due to fly to America to conclude another arms deal and that was far more important to him. Once in Washington, the Palestinians were quickly forgotten, until one night the National Security Adviser, Colin Powell, told him that he had 'seen something' on the news Rabin might care to look at. The 'something' was rather disturbing television footage of Israeli soldiers shooting at stone-throwing Palestinians, mostly youngsters. Rabin reportedly became slightly uneasy, but decided against an early return, still believing that the so-called uprising was only a flash in the pan. Upon his arrival in Israel he was met by journalists who eagerly awaited his assessment. From the start he made it clear that Palestinians would achieve nothing by violent means, saying 'Therefore, the main problem is to enforce order, with all the sorrow and pain over the loss on the Arab side. Whoever goes to violent demonstrations is placing himself in grave danger.'[154] With his recommendation of the use of force he was at odds with Shimon Peres who by then favoured a political solution, but closer to Prime Minister Shamir who approved of the draconian measures Rabin employed to quell

116

the uprising. Neither the random use of brutal force nor the detention of thousands deterred the Palestinians, and after only a month it became clear that neither Rabin nor the rest of the government had any idea how to deal with the situation.

The political establishment and its military personnel were completely at odds over what to do, with the former blaming the army for being too soft, and the latter being concerned about the army being sent into action despite deep divisions among the Israeli public over the way the IDF was employed and what military action was to achieve. A good illustration of the differences was Minister for Arab Affairs Ezer Weizmann's reaction to the disturbances in Gaza which he thought could be brought to a halt by getting the IDF 'out of Jebalya and let them burn each other'. When Rabin learned of Weizmann's remark he snapped back, 'what are you talking about? They will burn Jebalya, and then the fire will spread everywhere!'[155] Yet many politicians did not end their complaints against the military and made snide remarks insinuating that 'leftist generals' avoided ending the uprising because 'it vindicated their political philosophy'.[156] The Head of Central Command, Amram Mitzna, was a particular thorn in the side of right-wing politicians. Already in the past he had denounced settler violence against Palestinians and continued to remind his officers 'that in subduing the uprising Israel could not afford to alienate the Palestinian population completely or prejudice future negotiations towards a political settlement' and he pointed out that the army could only deal 'with the symptoms of the Intifada, not with its causes'.[157]

The Israeli public was shocked and dismayed: Israelis had believed in their 'benevolent occupation' and gotten used to travelling to the territories to visit Palestinian dentists, shop in the Old City in Jerusalem or take a stroll through Ramallah on Shabbat when the Jewish towns were empty and deserted. Suddenly these towns and villages Israelis had grown accustomed to since 1967 became virtual no-go areas, their cars were attacked by stone-throwing children, and their fathers, husbands and brothers in the army were fighting not a regular army but civilians armed with nothing but their anger and desperation, stones and later petrol bombs. Every evening television brought the gruesome pictures of Israeli soldiers brutally lashing out against Palestinian civilians into every living room in Israel and abroad. And no matter how much Israel complained that the reporting was biased and did not reflect reality, it could not stop international criticism and growing world-wide sympathy for the Palestinians. Rabin, albeit convinced that the army could not solve the problem, suffered no pangs of conscience. Whenever he appeared on television or was interviewed for radio programmes, he did not tire of repeating that Palestinian violence would be met with force, even if that meant using live ammunition.

During a visit to a detention camp at Ketziot in the late 1980s, Rabin was shown the kitchen where two Palestinians were peeling potatoes for lunch. It is said that he asked the men whether they really wanted to be behind barbed wire, implying that if they only would see the pointlessness of their resistance they could go back to living normal lives. The Palestinians' answer was that even if Israel incarcerated all Palestinians, they would still demand and one day get their state. Because, said the man, they simply had nothing to lose. Rabin said nothing. Most likely he puzzled over the hopelessness of Palestinian resistance in the face of one of the mightiest armies in the world and their unending fight.

Despite the obvious disruption the Intifada caused, Rabin did not take the Palestinians' actions as a serious threat. According to his wife Leah the Intifada never caused him a sleepless night; it was an embarrassment, yes, but not a danger.[158] But he grew increasingly impatient with the ineffectiveness of the measures he had ordered, and he had to concede that he had badly misjudged Palestinian stamina and the impact seeing their soldiers shooting civilians had on the morale of the Israeli public. And slowly Rabin became the target of many politicians' scorn. Already in spring 1988 they had shifted their contempt from the generals to the Defence Minister and began 'portraying Rabin as the real culprit for failing to make the army act more forcefully'.[159] Which was true in the sense that it was Rabin, and not the General Staff, who had the overall responsibility for the Israeli campaign against the Intifada. The so-called Territories Forum was composed of several military, police and secret service members and headed by Rabin.

In his usual efficient and thorough way, Rabin made himself familiar with the smallest details and followed up all his decisions and orders. He was responsible for a massive influx of Israeli soldiers into the territories – now that it was obvious that the occupation could not be upheld by the former skeleton force – where many Israelis came for the first time into direct contact with the harsh realities of Palestinian everyday life. Commercial strikes by the Palestinians were first met by enforced openings of shops, then shutters were welded closed and finally the army ignored them. Punitive measures were introduced, deportation orders were issued, demolition of houses and, once Palestinians started to throw Molotov cocktails, Rabin – who otherwise had given the generals a free hand to do whatever they thought fit – issued explicit orders to shoot anyone so doing.

One of his most infamous orders was that to beat demonstrators after shootings had caused complaints. During a visit to the troops, he reportedly advised Israeli soldiers to break Palestinian bones in order to drive home to the Palestinians that Israel would not succumb to their protest. In January 1988 Rabin reportedly told IDF officers in Gaza: 'Be more aggressive, but not with rifles. Beat them during a demonstration, but not otherwise'. In another meeting he said that Palestinians demonstrations should be met with 'force, power and blows. The first priority is to prevent violence in whatever form it takes, and by force, not by fire.'[160] He consistently denied this order two years later when a commission of inquiry into the responsibility of politicians for army abuses during the Intifada was proposed. But the words stuck and reinforced his image as a hawk. The result of this policy was even more devastating: the soldiers, already under strain by having to fight this unconventional war, released their pent-up tension and frustration during violent beatings and often literally followed Rabin's recommendation and broke bones with the help of rifle butts, stones and kicks. Once pictures of those savage beatings were seen by a national and international audience, Israel's reputation was further damaged while the Palestinians' plight was met with compassion. Rabin had to realise that he was losing this war and public opinion. In a television interview he admitted that 'I had believed that shooting would appear much worse in international opinion than the use of the . . . riot baton . . . I was surprised to discover that the sensitivity of world opinion to blows and physical confrontation was greater than to that of shooting.'[161] The introduction of rubber-coated bullets could salvage neither Israel's nor Rabin's reputation: the label of a cruel and brutal Minister of Defence who used force to cover up his failed policies and who seemingly took pleasure in the suffering of the Palestinians stuck.

But Rabin could not have taken any pleasure in Palestinian suffering since he did not harbour any feelings of hatred for them. His intransigent approach and insistence that the uprising was an annoying but manageable security problem was simply due to his basic understanding of how the conflict should be approached: by force. Only gradually did he come round and admitted that 'I've learned something . . . among other things that you cannot rule by force over one and a half million Palestinians.'[162] The Intifada proved to be his school at the end.

However, 1988 also proved crucial in another respect: during the Arab League summit in Algiers in June, King Hussein of Jordan unexpectedly absolved himself from any responsibility for the West Bank and announced that he would no longer negotiate on behalf of the Palestinians. It was Israel's worst-case scenario: they would have to talk to the Palestinians directly. Furthermore, and equally alarming for Israel, Yassir Arafat had renounced terrorism, pledged to accept UN Resolutions 242 and 338 as the basis for peace talks with Israel under the aegis of an international peace conference, and called for the mutual recognition of Palestinian and Israeli rights for peace and security. The international community, disturbed by Israeli handling of the Intifada and in response to Arafat's initiative – condemned by Israel as a 'deceptive propaganda exercise'[163] – rewarded him with goodwill and recognition.

The Intifada was the dominant theme during the next general election in November 1988. Labour was campaigning for a political solution and an exchange of territory for peace, whereas Likud promised even more of the (so far unsuccessful) 'iron fist' policy. The people, just as undecided as the politicians about what to do, gave neither Likud nor Labour a clear mandate. Since Likud had gained one more seat than Labour, Shamir was called on by the President to form a government. Due to a lack of a viable alternative, Shamir chose Labour again but this time there was no rotation of Prime Minister; Yitzhak Rabin remained as Minister of Defence.

The pressure on Israel, however, did not decrease. The Palestinians were more united than ever by Israeli repression and a growing wind was blowing from the United States which had agreed to enter into a dialogue with the PLO. The newly-inaugurated President George H Bush expected Israel to respond to Arafat's offer. So Shamir, who had no intention of talking with a 'terrorist organisation', offered his 'peace plan'. It was in fact Yitzhak Rabin's. Knowing that a Jordanian solution was no longer an option, Rabin knew that Israel had to talk with the Palestinians directly and that the current situation required the inclusion of a political strategy alongside a military one. By January 1989 he proposed a four-stage plan that included an end to the Intifada, a prolonged period of quite, subsequent elections among the Palestinians in the territories and negotiations with the elected Palestinian leaders as well as with Jordan for provisional Palestinian autonomy and final talks on the status of the territories. He hoped that the election would provide Israel with more acquiescent Palestinian leaders and warned the Palestinians that a refusal would result in more suffering for them. But Rabin's initiative, which was supplemented by harsher measures on the ground, had several shortcomings: it excluded the PLO and neither mentioned an Israeli withdrawal nor a Palestinian state. The US was pleased with the Israeli initiative and believed that it was a workable plan, even though it thought it did not go far enough. Yet, for the precise reasons that Shamir was able to accept Rabin's plan, the Palestinians rejected it, insisting that no agreement could be reached without the PLO. Consequently, the 'Shamir plan', and a further peace initiative launched by the successor to the murdered Anwar Sadat (Sadat, who was much less popular in Egypt than in the West due to his economic policies, his rapprochement with Israel and the yet unfinished business concerning the promised Palestinian autonomy within the framework of Camp David, had been assassinated by a Muslim group), the Egyptian President Hosni Mubarak, either came to nothing or were consistently fought over. Israeli infighting increased and was matched only by rising American frustration with Israeli intransigence. By 1990 the Americans had finally had enough and President Bush declared his opposition to further Israeli settlements in all of the occupied territories. Shamir could not have cared less and responded by publicly declaring that he intended to settle as many of the new immigrants – who at the time were coming in their hundred of thousands from the former Soviet Union – there as possible. Eventually Peres asked for the dissolution of the Unity government on the grounds that it 'is not trying to advance the peace process' and Shamir had 'no choice but to terminate [Peres'] service with the Government'.[164] After the other Labour ministers tendered their resignations and successfully carried a motion of no confidence, Shamir was voted out of office. Now it was Peres' turn to form a new government. Rabin was not pleased with this: he had prospered in his new office and still loathed any political gains by Peres. In an interview on 5 March, shortly before the government broke down, he noted that there are 'some in

Labour who seem to be in a great rush' to bring the current government down 'and it isn't the peace process which is their paramount priority, but something quite different'.[165] He believed that any government was better than one led by Peres. What followed were five strenuous weeks during which Peres, by coaxing, financial promises and political rewards, desperately tried to find enough parties to set up a government. The extent of his willingness to bend over backwards to preside over his own government not only infuriated the Israeli public – who at first watched Peres' deal-making and financial promises to the religious parties with disbelief and then demonstrated in the streets against his misuse of public funds to buy himself a government. But it was all in vain: on the day he presented his government before the Knesset, two members of a small religious party abstained from supporting Peres and he lost his majority; it was a devastating defeat. Rabin only called it 'ha Targil ha' Masriach', 'the stinky manoeuvre'. It must have been particularly galling since he had, unlike in the past, actively campaigned for Peres and even paid a visit 'hat in hand' to influential religious leaders to this end. Thus a few weeks later, while Shamir set up a right-wing government, Rabin announced that he would, yet again, challenge Peres for the party leadership.

Struggling to the Top Again:
1990–1992

A political commentator at the time noted that as a result of Peres' dealings, 'the political system has been raped, robbed, bruised and brought to prostitution'; it was the best possible background to Rabin's campaign, and his confidence was further boosted by opinion polls that predicted a comfortable victory for him if there had been general elections then and his opponent was Yitzhak Shamir. Peres, naturally, was not happy about yet another showdown, especially not two years before the next election, but he was willing to take up the challenge. A few days before the party contest he dryly said that he 'did not invite Rabin to a duel . . . But if he asked for a duel, he'll get it'.[166] Peres managed to turn up the heat and on 22 July, speaking in front of the party committee, he accused Rabin not only of slandering him and calling him names but also of having been involved in his failure since he had been informed of every step he took and neither in private nor in public ever objected to his efforts. Even though Rabin had previously accepted some responsibility, due to his 'main mistake' of preferring 'inner-party peace above other issues',[167] he was still confident that the party would support him. But he was wrong: the party wanted Peres. What eventually turned his luck was Labour's strive for greater democratisation in the aftermath of Peres' failure; the Central Committee decided to adopt American-style primaries for choosing its next candidate for the premiership.

On 24 December Rabin began his attempt to win the party's nomination for prime minister. He was the most popular politician at the time and knew that, apart from the party officials, rank-and-file members preferred him. In addition, the Shamir government ran into serious problems. Its last years were dominated by two major events: the unprecedented arrival of new immigrants and the Gulf War. The slow implosion of the USSR led to waves of Jewish immigrants leaving for Israel. They feared continuing anti-Semitism and wanted to escape the political and economic instability and, since the Americans restricted their immigration to the US, they came in droves to Israel. At the beginning they did not mind the difficulties they faced, like inadequate housing and poor job prospects, but their absorption was simply too much for a country at war that was struggling economically. Soon the newcomers' dissatisfaction grew and Shamir, who had previously claimed their arrival as his personal victory in Israel's unremitting struggle for Jewish immigration, had to realise that what was been intended as a political asset had turned into a liability.

The other major development was the 1991 Gulf War against Iraq. Israel, even though it was attacked by Iraqi Scud missiles, kept its promise to the United States that, in return for substantial financial aid which Israel needed for the new immigrants, it would not retaliate so as not to upset the carefully assembled US–Arab alliance for the liberation of Kuwait. At first Shamir's reticence seemed to pay off: Rabin, having been the Defence Minister for so many years, was seen as the main culprit of Israel's failure to prepare for such missile attacks and Shamir's popularity rose. But then the Americans, believing that the time was right, renewed their efforts to resolve the Arab–Israeli conflict. The Palestinians were at an all-time low: they had badly misjudged the political situation and backed Saddam Hussein, and thus were neither able to dictate the terms of nor the shape renewed negotiations would take. Furthermore Syria, Lebanon and Jordan had agreed to an international peace conference and direct talks with Israel. The Israelis had, thanks to American intervention, one of their main concerns, the Iraqi military, removed. However, the Israeli government was reluctant to agree. It was only the possibility that the US might withhold the desperately-needed loan guarantees they had promised that finally made Shamir agree to the so-called Madrid Conference.

The talks were based on previous UN resolutions and the Camp David Accords. The Palestinians, who were part of the Jordanian delegation and not members of the PLO, agreed to provisional stages for deciding the fate of the territories but insisted that eventually a Palestinian state should be established. Not surprisingly this was not what Israel wanted. Shamir later freely admitted that he had agreed to Israeli participation with the intent 'to drag out talks on Palestinian self-rule for ten years while attempting to settle hundreds of thousands of Jews in the territories'.[168] This rigidity and intentional foot-dragging cost Shamir dearly: the Palestinians translated their frustration into intensified violence within Israel, and America, incensed by Israel's settlement drive as well as political obstinacy, imposed sanctions on Israel and withheld the promised billions of dollars. Shamir reacted by building even more settlements in the occupied territories, but it backfired: the Israeli public was worn out by years of the Intifada, frustrated by high unemployment and an economic slump to which the Intifada had contributed, and the government investing money in the, in every respect, extremely expensive settlements in the territories.

Rabin sensed the growing discontent among the public and used it wisely: instead of only attacking Peres in his bid for the party nomination he concentrated on the increasingly embattled Shamir who had to fend off growing criticism from his own party and his coalition partners for, among other things, his opposition to electoral reform which the country had been demanding ever since Peres' unsuccessful attempt to buy himself a government. Eventually Shamir had to watch helplessly as his government unravelled and was forced to call for early elections within six months, in June 1992.

In his campaign for the leadership, Rabin relied on numerous volunteers, direct mailings and addressing small audiences in his usual awkward and matter-of-fact style. His campaign manager Ephraim Sneh knew that Rabin was 'neither Mr. Warmth' nor would he spontaneously 'wade into a crowd and kiss babies',[169] so instead he presented Rabin as the only one who could win the crucial votes for a Labour victory and emphasised his leadership qualities – and leadership was what the Israelis wanted – and his hawkish reputation and yet his willingness to work for territorial compromise. The no-less intensely campaigning Peres he branded a dove; not a compliment in a country which associates dovishness with general political weakness. His strategy slowly paid off and Sneh could see how Rabin eventually relaxed and gradually warmed to the crowds. And despite a temporary loss of voice and an enforced abstinence from smoking, Rabin's inherent pessimism gave way to the belief that he could actually make it.

The first primaries ever held in Israel took place on 19 February 1992. Yitzhak and Leah voted in the early afternoon in Tel Aviv after Rabin had urged his campaign workers to work till the last minute and then retreated to their home. He needed 40 per cent of the party's vote but right up to the end it was a tight race between him, Peres and two other candidates. In the end Rabin won 40.59 per cent, Peres 34.80 per cent and the two other candidates the rest. If it had not been for them, Rabin might well have lost.

But the real task was running for the national leadership, an option as Rabin called it, not an obsession. He intensified his campaign, criss-crossed the country and addressed weary Israelis who were tired of Likud, fed up with the political deadlock, fearing for their jobs, worn out by the Intifada and desperate for change. And Rabin promised change: while highlighting Likud's failures and holding it responsible for creating a 'erroneous and distorted order of priorities' in which 'political settlements in the territories precede everything else: immigration absorption, the future of the younger generation, the war against unemployment, and social economic progress' he pledged that 'should I form the next Israeli government I undertake to reach an agreement with the Palestinians in the territories over the establishment of autonomy within six to nine months. After the agreement with the Palestinians we shall reach an agreement with Jordan and then with Syria. The second thing which I undertake is to stop the settlements, whose only purpose is to prevent any possibility of finding a political solution to the conflict'.[170] This rather conciliatory tone he counterbalanced by portraying himself as a strong leader who did not give anything away for nothing and whose overall concern was Israel's security: 'I am unwilling to give up a single inch of Israel's security, but I am willing to give up many inches of territory – as well as 1,700,000 Arab inhabitants – for the sake of peace. That is the whole doctrine in a nutshell. We seek a territorial compromise which will bring peace and security. A lot of security'.[171] He successfully managed to downplay the similarities between Labour and Likud – like their mutual opposition to Palestinian nationalism, their denial of the Palestinian right to self-determination and the establishment of a Palestinian state – and instead presented the upcoming election as a chance for a new beginning and a break with the stand-off of the past.

Labour's whole strategy focussed in the end on the personality of Yitzhak Rabin, trying to take advantage of his popular appeal, military credentials and the tendency of Israeli voters to blame the parties *per se* for the country's ills. Thus they launched a campaign jingle with the catchphrase 'The people are waiting for Rabin' in imitation of the popular war song of 1967. When Labour celebrated the 25th anniversary of the capture of East Jerusalem, banners with Rabin's picture went up and he re-enacted his victorious entrance into the city. The message Labour wanted to put out was that the Israelis should vote for the Chief of Staff of 1967, the Prime Minister who signed an interim agreement with Egypt and under whose command the hostages of Entebbe had been freed, and lastly the Defence Minister who organised Israel's withdrawal from Lebanon.[172] Faced with such a personalised campaign Likud countered with attacks on his character, highlighting his breakdown when Chief of Staff and spreading the word that Rabin had a drink problem. Rabin immediately responded to the first charge, saying that he had nothing to hide and had already admitted to a bout of depression at the time but dismissed the second one as pure nonsense. It was well known that Rabin liked a drink, but no one ever saw him drunk. The rumour stuck but nothing was proved and it did not affect his campaign.

The election was held on 23 June. Rabin had been campaigning till the end and decided to await the result with Leah, his children and grandchildren at home. At 10 o'clock the news announced Rabin's victory by the single Hebrew world 'Ma'apach': 'upheaval'. After 15 years out of office, a landslide victory made Yitzhak Rabin Prime Minister again, enjoying a rare second chance at the age of 70.

A Second Chance: 1992–1995

The first thing Rabin did was to take the lessons of his first premiership to heart: after forming a centre-left coalition government that broke with its hawkish predecessor, he asserted his authority by doubling as Defence Minister and, not being able to do without Peres, gave him the Foreign Affair Ministry, but only after having made it quite clear to him that he, Rabin, was in charge of the overall direction of policy. Rabin presented his government on 3 July. As expected he reaffirmed his election promises but surprised everyone by challenging one of the most fundamental beliefs of the country: 'No longer are we necessarily "a people that dwells alone", and no longer is it true that "the whole world is against us". We must overcome the sense of isolation that had held us in its thrall for almost half a century'.[173] The acknowledgement that Israel was not alone also included the Arabs, most notably the Palestinians. His speech not only marked a clear break with the cultural paranoia his many predecessors had expounded but it was the basis for what Rabin came to symbolise: The Oslo Peace Process.

Secret Talks made Public

Rabin's election went down well with the Arabs and Palestinians, and their hopes seemed justified in the light of several confidence-building goodwill measures Rabin initiated shortly after his election: he freed Palestinian prisoners, rescinded deportation orders and repealed a law from 1986 that had forbidden any contacts between Israelis and Palestinians affiliated with the PLO. It was not, he emphasised, a sign that he intended to enter into direct talks with the PLO, but he at least wanted to decriminalise contacts between the two sides. Despite a change in government, however, the ongoing Middle East peace talks reached a dead end: not only did Rabin retain Shamir's man Elyakim Rubinstein as head of the Israeli delegation – thus sending a mixed signal concerning his proclaimed change of attitude – but the positions of the Palestinians and Israelis were still worlds apart: the Palestinians demanded an end to occupation which Israel was not ready to do. In December 1992 the Palestinians were further enraged when Rabin announced the deportation of 416 Hamas activists to Lebanon after the murder of an Israeli border policeman.

Hamas, the Movement of Islamic Resistance, was founded shortly after the beginning of the first Intifada. It started as an organisation that was mainly engaged in social and religious affairs but soon became a political organisation which did not hesitate to employ indiscriminate violence against Israelis in order to achieve the 'liberation of Palestine', that is, the abolition of Israel and the establishment of an Islamic state. Hamas grew in strength and popularity during the Intifada and always stayed independent from the dominant and nationalist PLO. Hamas, whose basic tenant was the belief that Palestine is an Islamic

134

trust that no one has the right to surrender or negotiate over, began vocal opposition to Madrid and later Oslo. In order to end any reconciliation between Israel and the PLO Hamas supported, organised and justified many bomb attacks, and later suicide missions against Israelis, whether soldiers, settlers or civilians, which cost the lives of more than 70 Israelis from 1994 to 1995.

Rabin's decision to expel the Hamas activists, which came after an extremely violent winter where 50 Palestinians had been killed by Israeli troops and 10 Israelis by Palestinians, proved to be very popular domestically but caused the Arabs to suspend any further talks. Rabin was unfazed; the deportation was perfectly in line with his credo that while he was willing to talk with the moderates he would continue to fight the extremists, famously saying 'We will fight terror as if there are no peace talks and we will conduct peace talks as if there is no terror'.[174] Hamas, as was to be expected, responded with a wave of attacks against Israelis and Rabin, not one to be accused of being soft, reintroduced some policies from the early 1990s and reacted with the sealing of the borders of the territories to Palestinian workers, punishing nearly 120,000 families as a result.[175]

At about the same time the new American President Bill Clinton became involved. In contrast to the previous administration his was much less even-handed and much more lenient towards Israel's position. Not surprisingly Clinton's involvement, which mainly presented Israel's position to the Palestinians, did nothing to resolve the dead-end the talks had reached by summer 1993.

But there were other talks which seemed much more promising. Secret meetings between Israelis and Palestinians began in January 1993 near the Norwegian capital of Oslo. The gatherings were initiated by Yossi Beilin, Deputy Foreign

Minister and a close aide of Shimon Peres, and the Norwegian researcher Terje Rod Larsen. Beilin, a former journalist and lecturer in political science, had advocated for a long time direct talks with the PLO and pursued a strategy that entailed a return to the pre-1967 borders, the establishment of a Palestinian state, the dismantling of Jewish settlements and the concession of functional Palestinian control of East Jerusalem. For many years he had consistently repeated that the preferred Labour option of so many decades, Jordan, did not exist and that the basis of solving the Israeli–Palestinian conflict must be mutual recognition of both parties and that direct contacts with the PLO were essential and the only way to achieve this. Beilin had informed Peres quite early on about his initiative but so far not Rabin. He was afraid of his reaction, knowing that Rabin had no concrete ideas or long-term vision of the shape and final outcome of an Israeli–Palestinian agreement, but rather isolated aims which often contradicted each other. However, once the talks in Oslo became more promising, substantial and concrete and reached a point where more and more Israeli officials were included to work out a deal, Rabin finally had to be told. To Beilin's surprise, Rabin did not object to the talks but neither was he enthusiastic nor show much interest. But gradually he became more involved and assumed a more active role alongside Peres. Since the Palestinians reported back to Arafat and the Israelis to Peres and Rabin, the talks opened up an indirect channel between Israel and the PLO. When Beilin presented Rabin with the Declaration of Principles (DoP) and the Letters of Mutual Recognition, he feared that Rabin would reject them immediately. But again Beilin was in for a surprise: Rabin just said 'OK. I am willing to co-operate, let's check it carefully and if it's possible, let's go for it'.[176]

His decision to accept the PLO as the representative of the Palestinians, as stated in the DoP, and thus a negotiating partner for Israel, was a decisive and courageous act. But his changed attitude and new willingness to accept the Palestinians as a partner of sorts – only after the PLO had made a series of concessions which went way beyond Israel's simple recognition of the PLO – was based on his careful calculation of the changed internal and external political and social circumstances at the time. In numerous private conversations he mentioned how he had to come to realise that the Intifada had wreaked havoc in the collective Israeli psyche. He saw worrisome signs of deterioration of morale in parts of the IDF and feared that the uprising had not only marred its reputation but also damaged its fighting spirit after it had been deployed as some kind of police force in the territories and forced to fight a war against a civilian population and not a proper army within the rules of a conventional war. Concerning the Israeli public, he saw the birth and expansion of peace groups that called for the end of the occupation and pilloried their government for the pointless deaths of more than 1,080 Palestinians and 100 Israelis during the Intifada alone.[177] He sensed weariness and softening among the Israelis which he found troublesome and which he feared might leave Israel unprepared and unfit for the conflicts which he was sure were still to come. He was particularly appalled by the behaviour of many Israelis during the Gulf War, who, instead of staying put and braving the storm, had fled the big cities or even the country itself. To him this was a sign of serious weakness and a dangerous flaw in a public that refused to stand by its country no matter what.

Concerning the international framework he applied his rather superior ability of clear-cut analysis and came to the conclusion that striking a deal now would best serve Israel's interests. The end of the Cold War had left the United States as the only super-power whose support was nonetheless crucial. Since Israel had benefited considerably from the conclusion of the Camp David agreement, there was no reason to believe that this could not be repeated. In addition he feared that the weakened PLO – which was at an all-time low politically and economically – might lose its fight against the Islamists for the national leadership and the idea of having to deal with the ideological and religious fanatics of Hamas was much less appealing than dealing with Arafat. Lastly he was intellectually honest enough to acknowledge that Israel simply could not afford to hold on the territories forever: the occupation was not only too costly, it was also, due to the higher birth rate of the Palestinians, seriously undermining Israel's aim of being a Jewish state. It was on this basis that he decided to go for Oslo and to try to solve the conflict by diplomatic rather than violent means. It was born out of pragmatism, not out of a sense of justice or morality. That is possibly why his subsequent policies revealed a profound lack of vision, of historical perspective and a continuation of the past, of sorts, rather than a clean break from it. He remained, after all, a soldier who had set out to ensure his country's security and to prepare it for the things to come, not an elder statesman who had overcome his emotional prejudices and intellectual limitations and who would now lead his country into a new era where the notion of peace had been granted moral substance and where the two nations would not only acknowledge each other's existence but also their inherent equality.

Nothing, however, showed his ambiguity, his serious ideological, psychological and political problems in changing his attitude and his personal inhibitions towards his 'new partner' better than the ceremony for the signing of the DoP on 13 September 1993 in Washington. The Americans, aware of the secret Oslo channel but not of its substance, offered to host a signing ceremony once it became public. But Rabin desperately tried to keep it a low-key affair. He feared that a highly-publicised formal procedure would cause Yassir Arafat to attend, and he certainly did not want any television pictures that showed him and Arafat, the icon and symbol of either indiscriminate terrorism or the freedom fighter, in seemingly happy reconciliation. He was apprehensive that after years of vilification of the PLO and its leader, his political opponents would use it as an excuse to attack him, and he did not want to provide the embattled Arafat with a photo opportunity to present himself as a strong Palestinian leader.

Yassir Arafat had indeed come a long way. The man whom Rabin would from now on deal with and at times call a partner for peace, had managed to survive and establish himself as the unquestioned leader of the Palestinians. He was born on 24 August 1929 in Cairo into a merchant family. His father's families had ties to the Gaza Strip and his mother came from a distinguished family that claimed direct descent from the Prophet Muhammad. He spent some of his childhood in Jerusalem, had already demonstrated against the British at the age of ten in Egypt and fought in Gaza in the war of 1948. Back in Egypt he was active in the Palestinian student union and was elected as its head in 1952 and his thoughts and actions turned more on the cause of the Palestinians, which he wanted to organise and arm in their fight for their homeland. He gained a degree in engineering from Cairo University in 1957 and subsequently went to Kuwait for eight years, where he was able, thanks to the relative freedom of action which

Palestinians enjoyed there, to start his political career while working first as an engineer and later as an owner of a construction and contracting company. In 1959 he founded Fatah. Central to his new doctrine was that the liberation of Palestine as he saw it was primarily the business of the Palestinians themselves and not the Arab states, a daring thought at a time when pan-Arabism was predominant. Encouraged by the victory of the Algerian Revolution in 1962, he began preparations for an armed struggle against Israel, which was not a popular idea among the Fatah leadership. The establishment of the PLO provided Arafat with the opportunity to consolidate his power and influence and by 1965 Fatah launched its first raids into Israel. However, only after the war of 1967, when the Arab states had been yet again humiliated and defeated by Israel, did Fatah, which was condemned by nearly all Arab regimes, grow in popularity. Arafat, however, still had problems finding enough supporters in the West Bank for his 'Revolution Until Victory', where revolution did not mean the change of the socio-economic order but the liberation of Palestine by armed struggle. The majority of the newly-occupied Palestinians still put their hopes in the Arab states and Israel took firm measures against Fatah members and thus discouraged many from joining. By 1968 Arafat, also known by his *nom de guerre* Abu Amar, went to Jordan but was ousted again in 'Black September' in 1970, a turning-point that made him sanction terrorism by an offshoot of Fatah, the Black September organisation. Among their most notorious terrorist acts was the kidnapping and murder of the Israeli Olympic team in 1972 in Munich, Germany.

The events of 1974, when the PLO was recognised as the sole representative of the Palestinian people, its subsequent granting of observer status at the UN, showed his leading position, which was not questioned even after the PLO's enforced withdrawal from Lebanon. For many Palestinians he symbolised and 'promised a remaking of their state of dispersal, a settling of the great score with Israel, and a revenge for the injuries inflicted on them since 1948'. Particularly the way Arafat chose his appearance – unshaven, always in rumpled fatigues, wearing a traditional headscarf and carrying a pistol – reinforced and reflected the idea of many Palestinians that liberation would come only 'out of the barrel of a gun'.[178]

Only slowly, after several setbacks and internal and external upheavals, did Arafat arrive at a two-state solution. In his speech to the UN Assembly in Geneva in December 1988 – after the Palestinian National Council declared the independence of Palestine on the basis of UN Resolution 181 of 1947 – he declared his acceptance of Israel's right to exist, renounced terrorism and accepted UN Resolution 242. He was rewarded by the opening of 'substantive dialogue'[179] with the US which had had no contact whatsoever with the PLO since 1975. The US had promised Israel only to talk with the PLO once it recognised Israel's right to exist. Arafat's subsequent failure to reign in independent, yet affiliated Palestinian terror groups in the following years, the uprising of the Palestinians in the occupied territories and his particularly ill-judged support for Saddam Hussein during the Gulf War in 1991 seriously weakened his position and Oslo seemed to be a chance for him to take the initiative once more and to deliver to his people what he was ultimately working for: a Palestinian state.

Since the Americans insisted on inviting Arafat, Rabin suggested that instead of going personally he would send Shimon Peres. The Americans, having ended their isolation of the PLO, paid no heed to his wishes, sensing that any agreement that was to mean anything needed the main protagonists present. Rabin was dismayed and consulted with friends and family as to whether he should go or not. What he did not do was ask Peres, the man behind Oslo, to come along. Despite their new working relationship which functioned surprisingly well, old animosity and past hurt still figured prominently and would from time to time resurface. Both men had come a long way and the transformation of Peres was no less obvious.

When Peres had first heard of the Oslo talks he had already developed a European Union-style dream of 'a new Middle East' and strongly believed that a precondition for the realisation of his vision was a resolution of the conflict. He advocated peace in return for open borders and economic prosperity from which not only Israel but the whole region would benefit.[180] He was often mocked for this vision but he strictly held to it and his 'soft' approach complemented Rabin's 'security first' attitude. Slowly their relationship improved over the ensuing years. A close associate suggested, since the peace process brought so many honours, culminating in the Nobel Peace Prize which they received together with Arafat in 1994, it 'made it possible for the two of them to divide the spoils without either one feeling deprived'.[181] Yet, on the day Peres learned with considerable surprise and hurt that he was to be excluded from the signing ceremony, he threatened to resign if Rabin should excluded him from the signing of a historic document that he, after all, had 'fathered' much more than Rabin. Finally an emissary had to be employed and only after many trips between the homes of the two men a compromise was reached: they would both fly to Washington.

With the final preparations under way, there were two outstanding issues: Arafat's uniform and the customary handshake at such official gatherings. Since there was not much to be done about Arafat's choice of dress – apart from renaming his military uniform a 'safari suit' as one American half-jokingly suggested – President Clinton tried to convince Rabin of the necessity of a handshake and promised to do his utmost to prevent Arafat from giving Rabin the customary kiss; the mere thought of it caused Rabin considerable distress. Finally, Rabin gave in. Bill Clinton described in detail in his memoirs *My Life* how Rabin was taught by an aide to shake hands with Arafat while gripping his forearm at the same time, which made an exchange of kisses impossible.

On 13 September 1993, while Clinton, Arafat, Peres and Rabin were all lined up before going onto the lawn of the White House, Arafat reportedly greeted Rabin and stretched out his hand. Rabin, firmly clasping his hands behind his back, just snapped 'Outside!' and continued to ignore Arafat for as long as possible. Throughout his speech Rabin looked tense, sceptical and ill-at-ease. During the moment of the unavoidable hand-shake, over which a smiling Bill Clinton presided with out-stretched arms, a truly unhappy-looking Rabin quickly squeezed the hand of a man he found profoundly distasteful and his body language reflected his genuine unease. Rabin never fully over-came his reservations about Arafat. Throughout the coming years, however, he managed to establish a working relationship, whether it was out of an eventually-developed sense of appre-ciation as some claim, or whether it was due to the fact that there was simply no one else who could speak for and on behalf of the Palestinian people, remains an open question. What did not change, however, was Rabin's basic attitude towards a negotiated settlement of the Israeli–Palestinian conflict: he favoured cautious progress over definite decisions with Israel – that is, himself – controlling the terms of the negotiations and he had no intention of formulating at such an early stage the eventual outcome of the interim period. It was a 'let's see and wait what time will bring' attitude, quite unusual for an ex-soldier.

The Oslo Agreement

The document Rabin and Arafat had signed not only left the status of the PLO open but was more a timetable for negotiations than an agreement. It aimed at a step-by-step process with an ambiguous outcome which postponed the tackling of the most contested and controversial issues – like Jerusalem, the Palestinian refugees, borders and the future of Israeli settlements – at the end of an interim period of five years. Rabin was clearly in favour of such a provisional solution that left ample time and space to readjust and adapt policies to whatever time would bring. Whereas Peres preferred immediate discussion of the final outcome, Rabin countered that he needed time politically to build trust between the Israelis and the Palestinians after decades of antagonism and to overcome domestic opposition. Personally it certainly suited his utilitarian nature: dealing with today's reality rather than with tomorrow's many 'ifs' and 'maybes'. Thus, unsurprisingly his answer to peoples' queries about what would happen after the interim period generally was 'Why are you asking all these questions? Who knows what will be next?'.[182]

The Declaration of Principles for Palestinian self-government – 'a meeting point between an Israeli wish to compromise territorially and a PLO willingness to begin peace negotiations with such a compromise'[183] as one observer noted – laid down that within the next two months Israel would withdraw from the Gaza Strip and Jericho. Simultaneously a Palestinian police force was to secure internal security in the evacuated areas while Israel would retain responsibility for external security and foreign affairs. In the West Bank Israel committed itself to a power transfer in five spheres: education, health, social welfare, direct taxation and tourism. Israel and the PLO further agreed that elections were to be held in the West Bank and Gaza for a Palestinian National Council (PNC) which would then act as a quasi-government yet without control over defence and foreign affairs which would continue to be in Israel's hands. Within the next two years, while the IDF withdrew from all major Palestinian population centres, negotiations over a permanent settlement would be achieved and implemented, as stated in the document.

Nonetheless, the following months and years showed that the greatest underlying flaw of Oslo – the unbridgeable disparity in status of the signatories – did not make for fair and balanced negotiations. No matter how far the DoP was a breakthrough in the relationship between the two peoples it could not mask the most basic and fundamental differences between them – a state with a well-developed and modern society versus a political organisation and its occupied and destitute people – that were supposed to hammer out a common future that was acceptable to both. Not only was Israel from the outset the stronger party – a pre-eminence that was further augmented by the support of an inordinately Israeli-friendly American administration that suddenly started to call the occupied territories 'disputed territories' thus, at least verbally, prematurely 'ending' the occupation – both sides also nurtured differing perceptions of what Oslo was exactly supposed to deal with and consequently solve.

For the Israelis the agreement was supposed to only take care of the issues that had arisen as a consequence of the 1967 war. The Palestinians, however, wanted the effects of the war of 1948, that is the question of the Palestinian refugees, addressed and solved, not altogether surprising since the sole reason for the PLO's existence was to deal with problem of the Palestinian refugees who had lost everything as a result of 1948. A further but still closely related aspect concerned the 'permanent peace' that Oslo was supposed to establish on the basis of UN Resolutions 242 and 338. The Palestinians understood this to mean that Israel – as requested by the UN – would withdraw from all territory it had occupied in 1967. Israel, however, had never accepted this interpretation and contended that Israel should only withdraw from some of that territory.

Furthermore, the divergence in the status and political weight of the signatories was also reflected in the vague wording of the documents which left ample room for different interpretations and analyses which Israel for the most part managed to exploit to its own benefit. Over the following months many disputes arose out of the documents' unclear provisions that caused confusion, arguments and regularly resulted in unduly delays and the missing of deadlines. One of the disagreements, for example, centred on the exact size of the Jericho area which Israel was to hand over to the Palestinians – Israel only wanted to give up 15 square miles whereas the Palestinians insisted on 150 square miles. Or what was the true meaning of 'withdrawal'? Was it total, like the Palestinians wanted it to be understood, or was it merely a redeployment, that is moving Israeli troops from one area to another, possibly still within territory that was to be Palestinian, as Israel wanted it?

Since Israel still enjoyed overall authority over Palestinian affairs and controlled the territory in the midst of which the isolated Palestinian self-rule areas were embedded, Israel was able to refine and in a way expand its control over the Palestinians:

146

the various islands of limited Palestinian self-governance were now controlled by Israel from further off but no less efficiently. While Rabin gave internationally well-received speeches about the necessity of reconciliation between his people and the Palestinians, frequently calling himself a soldier for peace in the army of peace, his obsession with the perceived security needs of Israel did not cease and was still the backdrop of his every action. And in the name of security Oslo slowly turned into a repackaging of Israeli occupation and rule rather than the end of it.

A prime example of how Israel switched from direct to more remote control was the erection of checkpoints on roads between Palestinian areas which controlled and prevented the movements of the people. Within a year Israel had established at least 56 permanent military roadblocks – in addition to temporary roadblocks – that greatly hindered the free movement of Palestinians and their goods and at times made it impossible. Meant as a security measure to prevent terrorists entering into Israel proper – especially once Hamas began its suicide bombings – the checkpoints became a serious grievance for ordinary Palestinians. They were often held up for hours on end without any particular reason and frequently suffered from needless harassment and humiliation at the hands of Israeli soldiers; a treatment that was widely criticised by Israeli and international human rights organisations alike. Furthermore, these roadblocks stood in open contradiction of a sub-clause of Article 10 of the Oslo agreement that clearly stated that 'there shall be a safe passage connecting the West Bank and the Gaza Strip for movements of persons, vehicles and goods' which Israel declared would ensure 'safe passage for persons and transportation during daylight hours . . . but in any event no less than 10 hours a day'.

Israel also did not adhere to the provision that 'neither side shall initiate or take any step that will change the status of the West Bank and the Gaza strip pending the outcome of the permanent status negotiations' as stated in Article 31, clause 7. It was repeatedly breached by the building of new Israeli settlements and the expansion of existing ones. As a result the number of settlers rose from 114,900 in 1993 to 132,300 in 1995[184] and the land the Palestinians envisioned for their state was further diminished while Israel continued to reinforce its presence.

The growing gap between the provisions and promises of Oslo and the evolving reality on the ground allowed for a situation where the majority of Israelis sincerely believed that peace was on its way. They accepted without question that Israel had every intention and in fact was continually withdrawing from the West Bank and the Gaza Strip. The majority could not agree more with the changed political rhetoric, especially with the catchphrase 'land for peace': they were more than willing to give up land if there was no repetition of the Intifada, if there was only an end to this endless, painful and costly conflict that had dominated their state since before its inception. They did not wish to occupy anymore, to live as occupiers any longer and to continue to endure personal insecurity in the name of national security. They may have greeted the reappearance of Arafat and his entourage in Gaza City with some unease and apprehension, but they accepted the old enemy as the only partner to end decades of war and conflict. What the majority of Israelis either could not see or preferred not to see – for it was a hidden, an untold and whispered story, one that did not find its way on the main pages of newspaper but was buried in the opinion sections – was the story of the expanding Jewish settlements, of redeployment rather that withdrawal, the roadblocks, the bypass roads, the curfews and the slow yet steady hollowing-out of true Palestinian self-government with meaningless symbols of semi-statehood. This supposedly 'new reality' of emerging peace, however, was enough to mobilise the Israeli Right and to propel them to openly challenge Rabin and, as they saw it, his dangerous playing with fire and abandonment of the 'promised land'.

Rabin's leadership and political wisdom was openly put to the test on 25 February 1994. Baruch Goldstein, an American-born religious settler, shot and killed 29 Palestinians worshipping in the Haram al-Ibrahim Mosque in Hebron, a holy city for Jews and Muslims alike but with a Palestinian majority and a fervently religious Jewish minority. Rabin had been under pressure before to crack down on militant settlers and to eject them from predominantly Palestinian areas. But he had refused on the grounds that Israel was first of all not obliged to do so during the interim period and secondly he saw no need to confront his most ardent opponents any sooner than he had too. Yoram Peri, a former aide and now head of the Institute for Media at the Tel Aviv University, asked Rabin why he did not get rid of the settlers who so bluntly tried to derail Oslo. Rabin replied that he neither wished to create an internal opposition nor did he intend 'to give the Palestinians now more' than he absolutely had to, adding 'I am willing to work with them [the Palestinians] for a common future but they will have to work hard to get it',[185] thus betraying many of his public statements about Israelis and Palestinians being 'partners for peace'. Therefore, instead of taking 450 Jewish settlers out of Hebron in the aftermath of the carnage he placed 160,000 Palestinians under house arrest for 30 days; a 'security measure' which he frequently applied in the following months.

Many of his political supporters, friends and family called his supine reaction to the Hebron massacre his biggest political mistake since Oslo began. Yet, Rabin, by appeasing his foes in order to reduce the level of antagonism within Israel, was able to show to the Palestinians that it was still Israel who set the rules of the game and that neither logic nor common sense would stop Israel from doing what Rabin deemed necessary. Added to his apprehension of confronting the settlers head-on was his fallacious belief that once he had made up his mind, the people, too, would eventually arrive at the same conclusions and accept his decisions without objection. This certitude was born out of his style of governing that was very different from his first term as Prime Minister. He had indeed made true his pledge from his election speech: 'I will lead, I will navigate, I will decide'.[186] It had been chiefly aimed at Peres but it also expressed his confidence that the people would ultimately trust him enough not to question his policies and thus free him from the tedious task of explaining and justifying his actions.

The Israelis, however, started to seriously question his assessment, when, in response to the Hebron massacre, Hamas began deadly retaliation. Palestinian suicide bombers ripped through Israel, turning coffee shops, streets and buses into possible death traps, leaving the Israelis stunned and completely surprised. This terror campaign caused first fear, then anger, later translated into profound doubts about the wisdom of the Oslo process. For many ordinary Israelis there was no reason for this kind of horror, no logical connection – no matter how inexcusable Hamas' action was – between the terror of Hamas and Oslo. Furthermore, they had considerable difficulties in making the distinction between radical Palestinian groups like Hamas, which always opposed any reconciliation and never ceased fighting Israel and all Israelis with military means, and ordinary Palestinians who supported a rapprochement and had nothing to do with bombs and the cynically-planned murder of civilians; a blurring of lines that was furthered by government calls on Arafat to reign in the terror groups. All the Israelis could see was their government's public pledge and official commitment to peace.

However, not only did the average Israeli pay a high price, but so did the Palestinians. They were not only forced to shoulder the true cost of Oslo but they were also charged twice: by Israel and by Arafat. The joy, pride and hopes of the Palestinians, who for the first time in their collective history saw their dream of a state come true, were soon bitterly disappointed. Despite Israel's partial withdrawals, Arafat's return to Gaza City and the subsequent setting-up of the limited and provisional Palestinian Authority amidst jubilant cheers and celebration, the Palestinian's dream of independence and a better future was a short-lived one. Arafat, the symbol of the Palestinian struggle, did not come from Tunis to Gaza City alone in the summer of 1994. He brought with him old companions and cronies and soon allowed the establishment of a regime that fell awfully short of the hopes of the Palestinians for a democratic society. The coming months and years showed that corruption, nepotism and authoritarianism were to become the key features of Arafat's regime. The new political elite that rapidly emerged enjoyed a lavish lifestyle with fast cars and expensive villas at the most beautiful spots in the Gaza Strip while hundred of thousands of Palestinians still lived under appalling conditions in refugee camps. The new leaders were also unaffected by Israel's policies such as curfews and restriction of movement. This cream of the crop often engaged in semi-legal businesses that brought them great wealth, exploited ordinary Palestinians and alienated them

151

from the people they had pledged to work for. Furthermore, many of these illegal businesses were conducted with the knowledge and blessing of Israel. In the eyes of the Israelis, as one observer noted, the material well-being of Arafat's cronies was a good thing: it was in the end an 'incentive [for those Palestinians in charge] to continue playing by Israel's rules of the game. In fact, Israel provided these officials numerous privileges . . . so as to sweeten their living situations'.[187] It was a bitter experience for the Palestinians of the so-called 'inside' (as opposed to the 'outside', those who had spent their lives in exile and not in the occupied territories): they had endured years of occupation and had paid the price for their popular resistance but they were not the ones who profited from the latest political developments but Arafat's friends.

What further dragged down their living standards and daily life were constant Israeli demands on Arafat to clamp down on Palestinian opponents to the Oslo process. The Israelis pressed Arafat hard on the security issue and wanted him to set up various security organisations in order to free Israel from the thankless task of policing the Palestinians, making it quite clear that if he failed to do so Oslo would come to a halt. And the new Palestinian security services were far from squeamish: they regularly used excessive force to ensure that internal dissent was minimal and paid little attention to collateral damage to freedom of expression and human rights. This in turn set ordinary Palestinians as much against their own National Authority as against Israel. It was a vicious circle whose mechanism was generally unnoticed by the Israeli public – though not necessarily by its political commentators and intellectuals – and successfully exploited by the Israeli government.

Rabin did not care much about the possible consequences of a people fighting on two fronts. He preferred the Palestinians to cope with the problem of enforcing order, knowing that there would neither be too much public outcry over excessive use of force nor appeals to the Supreme Court as he had faced when trying to quell the Intifada. In an infamous statement he said that Arafat could easily crack down on opponents since he could do so 'bli bagatz u'bli btselem' – without [the Israeli] Supreme Court or the [Human Rights organisation] B'tselem – looking over his shoulder.[188] This left many Palestinians with the uneasy feeling that the PA had replaced Israel as the new oppressor of Palestinian dissent.

Palestinian frustrations were further aggravated by the unceasing contradictions between Rabin's public statements and his policies; publicly he reasserted his desire to end 'the hatred' and to tear down 'the psychological walls', while at the same time he approved of the extension of settlements in and around Jerusalem and in several Knesset speeches pronounced on the right of the presence of existing settlements in the West Bank under Israeli rule and proclaimed that Israel would not return to the pre-1967 borders. Furthermore, Rabin continued to order internationally-condemned collective punishments: between 1993 and 1995 the number of closure days went up from 26 to 112 and the number of house demolitions was well above 100 per year.

Despite his ambiguous willingness to change the relations between Israel and the Palestinians, he pursued in his dealings with them a policy that paid little or no heed to Arafat's need to establish himself as an equal partner and that was insensitive to its devastating impact on the everyday lives of ordinary Palestinians. Yet at the same time it was a policy which was completely in line with Rabin's basic conviction that Israel's needs came first and that a solution of the conflict with the Palestinians would be essentially suited to Israel's wants and needs and consequently at the expense of the Palestinians. The interim period was for him a phase where Israel would secure its control over territory which it considered essential for its security and viability and not a trust-building period as he publicly said. The idea of a Palestinian state, which was widely discussed in newspaper editorials and grew in certainty and acceptability among the Israeli public, would remain a concept he could not accept. In a newspaper interview in October 1993 he already had said that 'there is nothing [in the accords] about a Palestinian state or a capital in Jerusalem . . . I don't believe there is room for an additional state between Israel and Jordan';[189] and in the following months he would only concede that eventually there would be some kind of a Palestinian entity, but one that would certainly be less than a state. Ironically, Rabin's tactic was not dissimilar to that of his predecessor, Yitzhak Shamir. Like Shamir he allowed for and in fact favoured protracted negotiations over procedures in order to consolidate Israel's position: the eventually favourable facts on the ground would ensure Israel's advantage during talks on permanent status.

But despite its mixed blessings Oslo continued and it rewarded Rabin and Israel with unprecedented international praise and diplomatic victories: in October 1994 Israel signed a formal and long-awaited peace treaty with Jordan, tourists started to return to Israel and international criticism of Israel made way for new honours, culminating in the presentation of Nobel price to Yitzhak Rabin, Shimon Peres and Yassir Arafat on 10 December 1994. But these were brief moments of respite and by mid-1995 no one could avoid seeing that Oslo, and with it Rabin, was in serious trouble.

The Final Mobilisation
of the Enemy Within

The national-religious camp had attacked Oslo from the beginning, but the Hebron massacre and the subsequent wave of Palestinian terror had a dramatically radicalising effect on it. The religious settlers saw no link between what happened in Hebron and the subsequent indiscriminate attacks on Israeli civilians. Instead they accused Rabin personally of having caused those deaths and charged him with bringing about a national disaster since he had recognised 'the terrorist organisation'. They organised countless demonstrations where furious settlers vented their mounting anger: shouts like 'Rabin is a traitor' and 'Rabin is a murderer' were common and sincerely believed. Then, after a rabbinical gathering, a large number of orthodox rabbis went one step further and directly challenged the government by telling soldiers that they should resist government orders when asked to evict settlers. Rabin was furious but could not put a stop to it. In 1995, after yet another series of Palestinian suicide bombings, the rabbis went one step further and blamed Rabin and Peres directly for the death of 87 and the wounding of 202 Israelis and explored the possibility as to whether Rabin could be deemed 'din rodef' and 'din moser'. According to Jewish law, the Halakha, both terms refer to a Jew who is committing acts of betrayal of the Jewish community which may result in the loss of Jewish life. Jews are obliged to kill a 'moser'. A 'din rodef' allows the killing of a Jew without any prior trial.[190] Even though none of the rabbis issued such a death sentence, their ruling created a highly charged and violent atmosphere where it was permissible to refer to Rabin as a 'madman' and 'a non-Jew', who is part of 'the vicious maniacs who run this government to take Jews as sheep to slaughter'.[191] Rabin, faced with these provocations and seeing the polarising effect it had on the social and political mood in Israel, stayed strangely aloof and detached. He well recalled the settlers' defiance in the 1970s and neither then nor now would he understand their sense of despair. In an interview at the time he just shrugged them off: 'If they think I am a traitor and murderer, I have no basis for any dialogue with them'.[192] Instead of putting them in their place he mocked them with open disdain; he called them 'cry-babies' and 'not real Israelis', admitting 'I feel contempt for them' and aggressively demanding 'Who are they? Have they fought in combat as I have?' when they accused him of jeopardising Israel's security.[193] Politically he countered their efforts to de-legitimise him by going ahead with the next step of Oslo: Oslo II, the expansion of Palestinian self-rule in major Palestinian villages and cities in the West Bank.

But there were also other segments of Israeli society which felt alienated by Oslo and who used it as a cover to voice their grievances. The socially and politically marginalised Mizrahi, the Jews from North Africa and other Arab countries who had come later to Israel than the founders of European origin (the Ashkenasim), had found a political home in Likud which had managed to present itself as an alternative to the Labour Party by appealing to their more traditional values and ethnic bases of their identity. With the beginning of Oslo, which also roughly marked the arrival of the adverse effects of globalisation in Israel, the economic gap in Israel widened and the losers were often the already-disadvantaged Mizrahi. Thus dissent against Oslo became a means for a general social protest against the Ashkenasi elite, and especially the secular peace camp, in their fight for social and economic equality which was epitomised in their protest cry that 'Peace is for rich Ashkenasim'. They joined an ever-growing popular opposition that reflected not only the immediate fear of terror attacks versus the long term benefit of peace, but also the difficulties Israelis had in coming to terms with the wider implications of Oslo.

As has already been said the Israeli public was initially in favour of Oslo. For many years they had questioned the wisdom and feasibility of prolonged occupation. If the return of land would bring them peace they were all for it. But the rise in Palestinian violence and the fact that the slogan of 'land for peace' challenged some of the core beliefs on which Israeli society was founded, and for which Rabin did not offer any substitutes, slowly eroded their support. Rabin's conflicting policies, his avoidance in defining the outcome and clarifying his aims did little to reassure the Israelis that peace would conform not only to their national values but was also in their interest. Rabin's assertion that 'only one who does nothing needs to explain' may have been perfectly in line with Ben Gurion's conviction that 'I do not know, nor am I interested in what the public wants. I know what the public needs'. This paternalistic approach might have been appropriate in the early years of the state, in a pioneer society, but was absolutely ly insufficient to meet the needs and ease the insecurities of a consumer and media society that was undergoing tremendous political and social changes. And his neglect of the public's anxieties left ample space for the growing alienation between him and his people; it was a void that was aptly exploited by one the most skilful political opponents he faced, the new leader of Likud, Binyamin 'Bibi' Netanjahu.

Netanjahu railed against Oslo not only on behalf of the Likud's traditional clientele but also expertly portrayed the government's policy in the face of terror attacks as deeply flawed and dangerous. He lent the dissenters his voice, stirred them up and added his respectability and political standing to the ever-increasing protests on the street. During a discussion of Oslo II in the Knesset on 5 October 1995, he berated Rabin in the Knesset, claiming that 'there has never been a government more removed from Israel's heritage' and 'a man should not give up his country and his home with that kind of ease and joy. Only one who feels like an invader and a thief behaves in such a fashion'.[194] Rabin dismissed his accusations with a wave of his hand.

The same evening thousand of right-wing demonstrators had gathered in Jerusalem's Zion Square following a call from the opposition parties. To the loud playing of patriotic songs, portraits of Rabin were burnt, people shouted abuse and called for his death. On the balcony overlooking the frenzied crowed stood several Likud politicians, among them Binyamin Netanjahu who cheerfully waved to the crowd. He began his speech amid cries of 'Bibi, Bibi', and throughout repeatedly questioned Rabin's legitimacy, called Oslo II a 'capitulation' and promised that, since 'the Jewish majority has not approved of the agreement' – Rabin had relied during the vote on Israeli Arab Knesset members – 'we will fight, and we will bring the government down'. When the crowds broke out in cries of 'Rabin is a dog' and 'in blood and fire we drive Rabin out', he did nothing to stop the verbal onslaught. The demonstration ended with shouts of 'Rabin is a Nazi' and the passing-around of leaflets that depicted him in a SS uniform.[195] After the demonstration was over, some protesters made their way to the Knesset that was still in session that night and lay in wait for Rabin. When they spotted his car driving towards the exit of the parking lot, they attacked it with fists and sticks; but the car was empty apart from Rabin's terrified driver. The Housing Minister, Binyamin Ben-Elezier, who witnessed this outburst of violence, immediately went into the Knesset and looked for Netanjahu. When he finally found him he warned him that he had 'better restrain your people. Otherwise it will end in murder'.[196] Netanjahu reportedly smiled uncomfortably and but insisted that he had neither been aware of the offensive posters and nor did he accept any responsibility for having incited the crowd. By then everyone in the Knesset had been informed of what had just happened. Its speaker, himself a Holocaust survivor, made a personal statement, expressing his disgust and calling upon all political leaders to condemn any reference to Nazism and the Holocaust in connection with the current political developments. Rabin angrily pointed at the opposition and asked 'what do you expect of them? They organised the demonstrations!'[197] The ensuing heated exchange between his supporters and his opponents, Rabin only followed from the hallway; accompanied by shouts of 'You're losing your wits', he had impatiently left the chamber for a cigarette break.

Only after he had been summoned three times by the Knesset's speaker did he return.

Following these incidents the peace camp finally reacted. It was more than obvious that Rabin was losing support for Oslo and that the Right was gaining valuable ground. It was decided that it was high time, after all the demonstrations by the Right, to hold a rally in favour of Oslo and to mobilise crucial support for the next steps of the agreement. Rabin did not like the idea. According to Yossi Beilin he thought it was premature: 'Why now? Once we need support we will get support'.[198] He also feared, being the pessimist that he was, that no one would show up, so by opposing the idea of a public demonstration he was trying to spare himself imminent and unnecessary disappointment. It took the concerted efforts of his political friends for him to agree and the date for the peace rally in Tel Aviv was eventually set for 4 November.

The events of the Zion Square demonstration and the ensuing violent clash at the Knesset car park was, even for Israelis used to heated and often unfair political debates, too much and seemingly had a quietening effect. But it was the briefest respite: a few days before the rally the incitement machine went into top gear again and the previous disgust for the Right's fanaticism faded. A death certificate with Rabin's name was circulating among settlers and demonstrations outside Rabin's home on the eve of the Shabbat became more and more hostile, deeply upsetting Leah. In an interview following his murder she recalled the events of the night before the rally. Amongst threats of 'next year we'll hang you like they hanged Mussolini and his mistress' she entered her home and waited for Yitzhak. After he arrived she asked him 'where are your people . . . why don't they drive them away? He only said:

"What can I do?" He tended to make light of them, not accord them any importance, not give them the satisfaction, of seeing that they managed to upset him'. But on that particular day he did make a telephone call, if only for Leah's sake: 'I don't pay any attention to them, and I don't care what they do to me. But I won't put up with the incessant affront to Leah's dignity'.[199] But the demonstrators had already returned home to celebrate the Jewish day of rest.

Among the men and women who had lain in wait for Leah was a young man called Yigal Amir. He was the son of Mizrahi Jews, Shlomo and Geula Amir, and had grown up in a mixed Ashkenasi and Mizrahi neighbourhood in Herzliya, near Tel Aviv. He went to a religious school and, after he completed his military service in 1993 (something he was very proud of since as a graduate of a religious school he could have applied for an exemption), he continued his religious studies and enrolled at Bar-Ilan University to study law and computer science. When Oslo became the new government's policy, he was surprised that Rabin, Israel's 'Mr. Security', had endorsed it; and was absolutely appalled when he watched him shaking hands with Yassir Arafat in September 1993. He had voted in the last election for the right-wing Moledet party, believed in the sanctity of the land and the mere thought of relinquishing Jewish land to the Palestinians was pure heresy to him. In a conversation at the time with his father, who was in favour of Oslo, he mentioned that it might be 'necessary' to 'take down Rabin'. A few weeks before this particular exchange had taken place, Amir had come across an anthology of articles written by Rabbi Yehuda Zvi Kook, the spiritual father of the religious settler movement after the 1967 War. Amir was less impressed by the recommendations of Kook than with the introduction which was written by the Rabbi and fervent settler, Benny Elon. Elon wrote that 'contrary to the secular activist approach, which holds that history is determined by man's action alone, . . . we must learn to fathom God's Will and "come to the help of the Lord"'.[200] From then on Amir, who had no doubt that Oslo was against divine will since the whole land was promised to the Jews, was obsessed with the means as to how God would tell him to carry out his will to destroy Oslo. He travelled to the settlements, took part in demonstrations against their evacuation and rallied support for them. He became part of the radical national religious camp that vehemently opposed Rabin and everything he stood for. The poisoned and violent atmosphere they had created and which part of the political opposition used to advance its own political agenda nurtured Amir's belief that the country needed a decisive act to stop a peace process that not only brought it close to civil war but contravened God's wishes for the Jews. The only act he believed would achieve this was 'taking down' Rabin. He tried altogether four times to do so, but always had either lost his nerve or received a 'sign that the time was not yet right'. But 4 November was to be the day where he would set out to obey God's will, not for 'revenge, or punishment, or anger, Heaven forbid' but for saving 'the Jewish people from destruction'.[201]

The Last Day: 4 November 1995

November 4th was a Saturday. Usually the Rabins played tennis with their friends at the Ramat Aviv Country club at weekends, but Rabin had to give it a miss since he had too many appointments and in addition, had woken up with an irritation in his eye. Leah arranged for a doctor to examine it and went alone to the tennis court. At nine Giora Eini came to Rabin's house. He was a trade union lawyer, seldom seen in public but a valued and important mediator between Rabin and Peres who still had to carefully balance their new working relationship at times. Halfway through their meeting a doctor arrived and gave Rabin some eye drops. After Eini left Rabin had another meeting with a financial adviser. At around 2.30 he left with Leah for lunch with friends and spent the rest of the afternoon napping. In the early evening he and Leah were picked up by their driver who drove them to the Malchei Yisrael square, the location of the peace rally. Rabin was still anxious that he would be embarrassed by his supporters not showing up but when he arrived he saw about 100,000 followers in the square. It pleased him enormously and he did not mind at all that his pessimism had been proven wrong. When he was led on stage among cheerful shouts of his name his face was uncharacteristically flushed with excitement and joy. When he finished speaking he received thunderous applause. Suddenly Shimon Peres appeared on stage and Rabin, moved and touched by the peoples' support, reached out and embraced the completely surprised Peres; it was the first time that Rabin had expressed any sign of affection for the man he had always scorned. The rally ended with the singing of the 'Song of Peace'. Together with the popular singer Miri Aloni, Shimon Peres and others, Rabin, 'painfully shy and unable to carry a tune'[202] sang the song that had been written in 1970 and which later, by the order of a political advisor under the premiership of Yitzhak Rabin in the 1970s, was banned from being played in the army.

After finishing the song, Rabin neatly folded the paper and put it in his pocket. The rally ended with the national anthem. Friends suggested that Rabin and Peres should go out and mix with the people, but the security service dismissed the idea as too dangerous; they feared a possible Palestinian terrorist attack. Thus Rabin decided to go straight home. Together with Leah he tried to make his way through the waiting crowds but eventually they got separated. 'Where is Leah?'[203] were his last words before two dum-dum bullets, fired by the 25-year-old Yigal Amir, entered his body. He was immediately pushed into his waiting car and his driver took him to hospital, asking occasionally how he was. His answer only minutes before he lost consciousness was: 'My back hurts, but it is not too bad'.[204] Yitzhak Rabin was pronounced dead shortly upon his arrival at the Ichilov hospital in Tel Aviv.

***

The murder sent waves of shock, despair and disbelief throughout the country and the world. Israel mourned his death like no one else's before: special television programmes were aired, hundred of thousands of people gathered spontaneously in front of his home and in the square, lightening candles and desperately trying to come to terms with his violent death. The fundamental divisions between the Israelis had not disappeared, but in the aftermath of the assassination they gave way to a collective soul-searching and a muted political discourse. Shimon Peres took over after Rabin's death but, neither willing nor able to capitalise on the murder, lost the next election to Netanjahu and the already ailing peace process came to an end. The most important consequence, however, was the transformation of Yitzhak Rabin: forgotten were his contradictory policies and his ambiguity towards Oslo. The mourning over his violent death, the missed chances and the crushed hope that maybe he would have turned things around transformed him into a myth 'who became a symbol in his death'[205] and thus the symbol for a peace that refused to materialise. Ironically he became in death what he was unable to be in life: a harbinger of a fundamental change that would finally bring about peace between Israelis and Palestinians.

Glossary

Ashkenasim: Assumed to be a corruption of the German
   allemagne. Originally it was used to describe Jews from
   Germany. Later it was extended and refers now to Jews
   from Europe and the US.

Betar: Acronym for 'Brit Yosef Trumpeldor', the Joseph
   Trumpeldor pact. Trumpeldor, a Israeli pioneer and soldier, became a military hero when, during a battle with
   Arabs, supposedly saying 'tov lamut be'ad artzenu' ('it is
   good to die for our country') shortly before his death.
   Betar itself was a youth movement closely affiliated with
   the Revisionist Ze'ev Jabotinsky.

Diaspora: Name given to the dispersal of the Jewish people
   throughout the world and to those Jews who still live
   outside Israel.

Gahal: Acronym for 'Giyus Hutz-Le'Aretz' (mobilisation

abroad), the Hebrew term for immigrant volunteers who arrived in Palestine during the late 1940s and who joined the Jews of the Yishuv (*qv*) in their fight for a state. Many of the volunteers had been survivors of the Holocaust, were interned by the British in Cyprus or gone through displaced persons' camps in Europe.

Gush Emunim: Hebrew for 'Block of the Faithful'. It is a Jewish fundamentalist group, that was founded in 1973. Its members claim the divine right to settlement of the West Bank, Gaza Strip, and Golan Heights as part of Israel. Its spiritual founder was Rabbi Kook the elder whose writing and thinking was both eschatological and messianic, assuming the imminent coming of the Messiah and the triumph of the Jews over non-Jews and their following rule over them.

Ha'aretz: Hebrew for 'the land' and the name of Israel's only broadsheet newspaper.

Hagana: Hebrew for 'defence'. It was a Jewish underground military organisation that was founded in 1920. Its successor is the Israeli Defense Force (IDF).

Hamas: Acronym for the Arabic word for 'Zeal', the movement of Islamic resistance. It was created by the Society of Muslim Brothers, a society which before mainly engaged in social and religious activities, shortly after the outbreak of the first Intifada. Its most notorious leader was Sheikh Ahmed Yassin, who was assassinated by Israel in March 2004. Yassin was strongly in favour of Hamas' active role in the uprising and later violently opposed subsequent peace negotiations like the Madrid Conference and the Oslo Accords. Hamas achieved notoriety once it employed bomb attacks and suicide bombers in what they perceived as legitimate tools in their struggle against Israeli occupation.

Herut: Hebrew for 'freedom'. Political party founded in 1948 whose undisputed leader was Menachem Begin. It was closely affiliated with Revisionism. Later Herut formed the Gahal bloc (acronym for 'Gush Herut-Liberalim', 'Herut-Liberal Bloc') with the Liberal Party. After internal party squabbles – which caused the departure of several party members – yet another new party was formed which eventually became the Likud Party (Hebrew for Union) in 1973 and exists today.

Histadrut: Founded in 1920 as the federation of Jewish labour. It was an all-encompassing federation which dealt as much with trade union affairs as it engaged in social activities which actively shaped the economic, social and political development of first the Yishuv (*qv*) and later the Israeli state and its society.

Intifada: Arabic for 'raising the head' or also referred to as 'shaking off'. It is the name the Palestinians gave their first and now second uprising against Israeli occupation of the territories which started on 7 December 1987 in the Gaza Strip. Its main features were collective civil disobedience, stone-throwing by Palestinian youths, demonstrations and strikes. It was a spontaneous outbreak of Palestinian frustration which only later on became more organised. Unlike the current Intifada it was less violent and rewarded the Palestinians with Western support.

Irgun Zva'i Le'umi (IZL, or Etzl): Hebrew, meaning 'national military organisation'. Founded in 1931, after an internal dispute within the Hagana (*qv*), it was an underground military organisation that was ideologically close to Revisionism. IZL pursued an activist policy which gained notoriety for its attacks against British institutions, most notably the bombing of the King David Hotel in Jerusalem and the hanging of two British sergeants in 1947. IZL also cooperated with Lehi (*qv*).

Kibbutz (plural Kibbutzim): Collective settlement. The first settlements concentrated on agriculture and the reconnecting of the Jew with his ancient land. The kibbutzim, following socialist ideas as well as the order of Zionism, propagated equality between the sexes, collective work and lifestyles and were instrumental in settling the land as well as serving as military outposts before, during and after the establishment of Israel. Nowadays kibbutzim are less egalitarian, pay their members a salary and do not have the importance they did in the past, when being a 'kibbutznik' was like being a member of some kind of aristocracy in Europe.

Kippa: is usually a knitted cap which religious Jews wear, particularly during visits to the synagogue or on religious holidays.

Knesset: Hebrew for 'assembly'. The Knesset is Israel's unicameral parliament and consists of 120 members. It derives its name from the first representative assembly after the end of Jewish exile in Babylon in the 5th century BCE.

Kvutza: Hebrew for 'group', plural Kvutzot.

Lehi/Stern Group: Acronym for 'Lohamei Herut Yisrael', 'Fighters for the Freedom of Israel'. Lehi was an underground Jewish terrorist group, which was also known as Stern Gang, after its founder Avraham Stern. It was formed by a group of IZL (*qv*) dissidents, after IZL decided to temporarily cease its attacks on the British in 1940. Lehi advocated the transfer of the Palestinians, sought contact with Germany and Italy in the hope that aid against the British might be forthcoming and was outlawed in 1948 after the assassination of UN mediator Count Bernadotte. Eventually service in Lehi was granted official recognition despite its terrorist past

Likud: *see* Gahal

Mapai: Acronym for 'Mifleget Poa'alei Eretz Yisrael' (the Party of Land of Israel Workers). This socialist Zionist party existed from 1930 till 1968. Its members later on merged with other parties and it was the forerunner of Israel's Labour Party. All Israeli prime ministers, all but one president and all Histadrut (*qv*) secretaries were members of Mapai.

Mizrahi/Sephardim: Both terms are sometimes – and incorrectly – used interchangeably. Yet, Mizrahi or more precisely Edot Mizrahi (Hebrew for Eastern/Oriental community), describes Jews who came to Israel from Arab Muslim countries, whereas Sephardim (Hebrew 'Spharad' means Spain, singular: Sephardi) were the Jews who lived in Spain until their expulsion in 1492. The Mizrahi Jews, who came to Israel after 1948, differed not only from the Ashkenasi (*qv*) and Sephardi Jews, but also had little in common with each other. However, they were equally treated and often looked down upon by the Ashkenasim, usually due to the fact that they were more traditional, that is more 'backward'. The issue of full integration versus alienation still plays an important role in Israeli society and politics.

Palmach: Hebrew for 'striking force, it was part of the Hagana (*qv*) and was established in 1941 as a full-time military force of volunteers to fend of German and Italian invasion. After the Second World War the Palmach became the principal force in the Yishuv's (*qv*) struggle against the British and later in the fight for the establishment of a Jewish state against invading Arab armies. It was disbanded in 1948.

Sabra (plural Sabres): Hebrew for native-born Jews in Palestine and later Israel.

Shtetl: Little city, town, or village. Often used to refer to the small Jewish communities of Eastern Europe.

Yishuv: the Jewish community in Palestine prior to the establishment of the State of Israel.

Notes

1. Dan Kurzman, *Soldier of Peace, The Life of Yitzhak Rabin 1922-1995* (HarperCollinsPublishers: 1998), p 47.
2. Walter Laqueur and Barry Rubin (eds), *The Israel-Arab Reader* (6th edition, Penguin Books: 2001), p 16.
3. Yitzhak Rabin, *The Rabin Memoirs* (expanded edition, University of California Press: 1996), p 5.
4. Kurzman, *Soldier,* p 51.
5. Rabin, *Memoirs*, p 6.
6. Interview with Rachel Rabin, Israel 16 June 2004.
7. Rabin, *Memoirs*, p 6.
8. Kurzman, *Soldier*, p 62.
9. Rabin, *Memoirs*, p 7.
10. Rabin, *Memoirs*, p 6.
11. Rabin, *Memoirs*, p 7.
12. Kurzman, *Soldier*, p 74.
13. Rabin, *Memoirs*, p 8.
14. Rabin, *Memoirs*, p 8.
15. Mark Tessler, 'Israeli Thinking about the Palestinians', in Robert O Freedman, *Israel's First Fifty Years* (University of Florida Press: 2000), p 96 ff.
16. Tessler, 'Israeli Thinking', p 102.
17. Charles D Smith, *Palestine and the Arab-Israeli Conflict* (5th edition, Macmillan Press: 2004), p 131.
18. Rabin, *Memoirs*, p 11.
19. Robert Slater, *Rabin of Israel* (revised edition, Robson Books: 1993), p 48.

20. Rabin, *Memoirs*, p 14.
21. Rabin, *Memoirs*, p 14
22. William L Cleveland, *A History of the Modern Middle East* (Westview Press: 1994), p 243.
23. Kurzman, *Soldier*, p 98.
24. Leah Rabin, *Rabin, Our Life, His Legacy* (G P Putnam's Son: 1997), p 44.
25. Leah Rabin, *Rabin,* p 57.
26. Rabin, *Memoirs*, p 35.
27. Rabin, *Memoirs*, p 17.
28. Rabin, *Memoirs*, p 18.
29. Rabin, *Memoirs*, p 19.
30. Avi Shlaim, *The Iron Wall: Israel and the Arab World* (Penguin Books: 2000), p 31.
31. Smith, *Palestine*, p 191.
32. Shlaim, *Iron Wall*, p 31.
33. Rabin, *Memoirs*, p 28.
34. Rabin, *Memoirs*, Appendix A, censored passage from his memoir's first edition.
35. Rabin, *Memoirs*, Appendix A.
36. Rabin, *Memoirs*, p 35.
37. Leah Rabin, *Rabin,* p 82.
38. Leah Rabin, *Rabin,* p 83.
39. Shlaim, *Iron Wall*, p 34.
40. Smith, *Palestine*, p 194.
41. Rabin, *Memoirs*, p 42.
42. Slater, *Rabin*, p 84.
43. Slater, *Rabin*, p 83.
44. Rabin, *Memoirs*, p 48.
45. Rabin, *Memoirs*, p 45.
46. Rabin, *Memoirs*, p 49.
47. Leah Rabin, *Rabin,* p 60.
48. Quoted in Slater, *Rabin*, p 104.
49. Rabin, *Memoirs*, p 50.
50. Leah Rabin, *Rabin,* p 94.
51. Kurzman, *Soldier*, p 178.
52. Efraim Inbar, *Rabin and Israel's National Security* (Woodrow Wilson Press: 1999), p 62.
53. Smith, *Palestine*, p 225.
54. Quoted in Smith, *Palestine*, p 225.
55. Ilan Pappe, *A History of Modern Palestine* (Cambridge University Press: 2004), p 161.
56. Pappe, *A History*, p 162.

57. Smith, *Palestine*, p 226.
58. Cleveland, *A History*, p 293.
59. Smith, *Palestine*, p 240.
60. Smith, *Palestine*, p 242.
61. Rabin, *Memoirs*, p 52.
62. Rabin, *Memoirs*, p 54.
63. Inbar, *Rabin*, p 64.
64. Rabin, *Memoirs*, p 54.
65. Personal interview with Gideon Levy, Israel, June 2004.
66. Alain Gresh and Dominique Vidal, *The New A-Z of the Middle East* (IB Tauris: 2004), p 249.
67. Rabin, *Memoirs*, p 57.
68. Rabin, *Memoirs*, p 59.
69. Shlaim, *Iron Wall*, p 230.
70. Slater, *Rabin*, p 114.
71. Rabin, *Memoirs*, p 64.
72. Rabin, *Memoirs*, p 71.
73. Rabin, *Memoirs*, p 76.
74. Rabin, *Memoirs*, p 81.
75. Rabin, *Memoirs*, p 83.
76. Quoted in John Quigley, *The Case for Palestine - An International Law Perspective* (Duke University Press: 2005), p 164.
77. Quoted in Quigley, *The Case*, p 165.
78. Shlaim, *Iron Wall*, p 250.
79. Rabin, *Memoirs*, p 102.
80. Rabin, *Memoirs*, p 112.
81. Rabin, *Memoirs*, p 119.
82. Slater, *Rabin*, p 148.
83. Rabin, *Memoirs*, p 122.
84. Laquer and Rubin, *Reader*, p 116.
85. Rabin, *Memoirs*, p 126.
86. Rabin, *Memoirs*, p 127.
87. Rabin, *Memoirs*, p 127.
88. Shlaim, *Iron Wall*, p 287.
89. Rabin, *Memoirs*, p 158.
90. Rabin, *Memoirs*, p 203.
91. Rabin, *Memoirs*, p 165.
92. Slater, *Rabin*, p 180.
93. Rabin, *Memoirs*, p 175.
94. Pappe, *A History*, p 193.
95. Slater, *Rabin*, p 185.
96. Leah Rabin, *Rabin*, p 135.
97. Slater, *Rabin*, p 189.

98. Quoted in Slater, *Rabin*, p 191.
99. Rabin, *Memoirs*, p 235.
100. Rabin, *Memoirs*, p 234.
101. Gresh and Vidal, *A-Z*, p 7.
102. Rabin, *Memoirs*, p 237.
103. Quoted in Leah Rabin, *Rabin*, p 146.
104. Smith, *Palestine*, p 335.
105. Rabin, *Memoirs*, p 241.
106. Rabin, *Memoirs*, p 240.
107. Rabin, *Memoirs*, p 242.
108. Slater, *Rabin*, p 227.
109. Rabin, *Memoirs*, p 303.
110. Rabin, *Memoirs*, p 303.
111. Rabin, *Memoirs*, p 303.
112. Quoted in Slater, *Rabin*, p 228.
113. Rabin, *Memoirs*, p 243.
114. Rabin, *Memoirs*, p 246.
115. Rabin, *Memoirs*, p 247.
116. Inbar, *Rabin*, p 85.
117. Shlaim, *Iron Wall*, p 329.
118. Shlaim, *Iron Wall*, p 334.
119. Shlaim, *Iron Wall*, p 336.
120. Rabin, *Memoirs*, p 262.
121. Rabin, *Memoirs*, p 271.
122. David Horowitz (ed), *Yitzhak Rabin - Soldier of Peace* (Peter Halban, 1996), p 62.
123. Smith, *Palestine*, p 324.
124. Rabin, *Memoirs*, p 287.
125. Rabin, *Memoirs*, p 288.
126. Rabin, *Memoirs*, p 289.
127. Rabin, *Memoirs*, p 289.
128. Rabin, *Memoirs*, p 306.
129. Rabin, *Memoirs*, p 311.
130. Rabin, *Memoirs*, p 312.
131. Mark Tessler, *A History of the Israeli-Palestinian Conflict* (Indiana University Press: 1994), p 505.
132. Rabin, *Memoirs*, p 314.
133. Slater, *Rabin*, p 306.
134. Shimon Peres, *Battling for Peace* (Weidenfeld & Nicolson: 1995), p 166,
135. Personal interview with Dalia Rabin-Pelosof, Israel, June 2004.
136. Quoted in Shlaim, *Iron Wall*, p 353.
137. Quoted in Tessler, *A History*, p 507.

138. Rabin, *Memoirs*, p 259.
139. Quoted in Kurzman, *Soldier*, p 370.
140. Rabin, *Memoirs*, p 322.
141. Rabin, *Memoirs*, p 323.
142. Rabin, *Memoirs*, p 329.
143. Rabin, *Memoirs*, p 331.
144. Rabin, *Memoirs*, p 331.
145. Rabin, *Memoirs*, p 332.
146. Quoted in Slater, *Rabin*, p 307.
147. Slater, *Rabin*, p 310.
148. Slater, *Rabin*, p 311.
149. Quoted in Slater, *Rabin*, p 313.
150. Quoted in Slater, *Rabin*, p 320.
151. Slater, *Rabin*, p 329.
152. Shlaim, *Iron Wall*, p 445.
153. Quoted in Slater, *Rabin*, p 335.
154. Yoram Peri, *Afterword* in Rabin, *Memoirs*, p 353.
155. Quoted in Slater, *Rabin*, p 338.
156. Ze'ev Schiff and Ehud Ya'ari, *Intifada* (Touchstone Books: 1989), p 11.
157. Quoted in Slater, *Rabin*, p 340.
158. Schiff and Ya'ari, *Intifada*, p 132.
159. Schiff and Ya'ari, *Intifada*, p 134.
160. Schiff and Ya'ari, *Intifada*, pp 135 and 136.
161. Quoted in Slater, *Rabin*, p 341.
162. Schiff and Ya'ari, *Intifada*, p 138.
163. Shlaim, *Iron Wall*, p 467.
164. Quoted in Slater, *Rabin*, p 353.
165. Shlaim, *Iron Wall*, p 471.
166. Slater, *Rabin*, p 360.
167. Quoted in Slater, *Rabin*, p 358.
168. Smith, *Palestine*, p 419.
169. Slater, *Rabin*, p 378.
170. Quoted in Slater, *Rabin*, p 387.
171. Quoted in Slater, *Rabin*, p 389.
172. Slater, *Rabin*, p 391.
173. Shlaim, *Iron Wall*, p 507.
174. Quoted in Kurzman, *Soldier*, p 465.
175. Shlaim, *Iron Wall*, p 510.
176. Personal interview with Yossi Beilin, Israel, June 2004.
177. www.btselem.org/English/Statistics/First_Intifada_Tables.asp, The Israeli Information Center for Human Rights in the Occupied Territories.

178. Philip Mattar (ed), *Encyclopedia of the Palestinians* (Facts On File Library: 2000), p 51.
179. Mattar, *Encyclopedia*, p 55.
180. Shlaim, *Iron Wall*, p 505.
181. Peri, *Afterword*, p 375.
182. Personal interview with Yoram Peri, Israel, June 2004.
183. Pappe, *History*, p 243.
184. http://www.passia.org/palestine_facts/pdf/pdf2004/6-Land-Settlements.pdf
185. Personal interview with Yoram Peri, Israel, June 2004.
186. Peri, *Afterword*, p 373.
187. Cheryl A Rubenberg, *The Palestinians* (Lynne Rienner Publishers, Inc: 2003), p 241.
188. Quoted in Rubenberg, *Palestinians*, p 240, compare also *notes*, p 277.
189. Quoted in Smith, *Palestine*, p 444.
190. Ehud Sprinzak, 'Israel's Radical Right', in Yoram Peri (ed), *The Assassination of Yitzhak Rabin* (Stanford University Press: 2000), p 108.
191. Sprinzak, 'Israel's Radical Right', p 111.
192. Television Documentary, *Israel's Generals: Yitzhak Rabin*, 2003.
193. Michael Karpin and Ina Friedman, *Murder in the Name of God* (Metropolitan Books: 1998), p 79.
194. Karpin and Friedman, *Murder*, p 93.
195. Karpin and Friedman, *Murder*, p 95.
196. Karpin and Friedman, *Murder*, p 97.
197. Karpin and Friedman, *Murder*, p 98
198. Personal interview with Yossi Beilin, Israel, June 2004.
199. Karpin and Friedman, *Murder*, p 101.
200. Karpin and Friedman, *Murder*, p 23.
201. Karpin and Friedman, *Murder*, p 27.
202. Peri, *Afterword*, p 340.
203. Leah Rabin, *Rabin,* p 10.
204. Peri, *Afterword*, p 340.
205. Peri, *Assassination*, p 182.

Select Bibliography

Life and Politics

Freedman, Robert O (ed), *Israel under Rabin* (Westview Press: 1995) – articles on Rabin's second premiership.

Horowitz, David (ed), *Yitzhak Rabin - Soldier of Peace* (Peter Halban: 1996) – comprehensive introduction to his life. Edited by the editor of the *Jerusalem Report*, an bi-monthly Israeli English-language magazine.

Inbar, Efraim, *Rabin and Israel's National Security* (Woodrow Wilson Center Press: 1999) – description of Rabin's impact on the Israeli army, his approach to international politics, including his American orientation, and his changing attitude towards the use of force.

Karsh, Efraim (ed), *From Rabin to Netanjahu* (Frank Cass: 1992) – gives a brief historical overview of the Israeli–Palestine conflict before it concentrates on Rabin's policy and the evolution of Oslo.

Karpin, Michael and Ina Friedman, *Murder in the Name of God* (Metropolitan Books: 1998) – account of the socio-political circumstances of his murder and his assassination.

Kurzman, Dan, *Rabin of Israel* (HarperCollinsPublishers:
1998) – rich in detail and well-researched biography,
slightly glorifying and written with hindsight.

Makowsky, David, *Making Peace with the PLO: The Rabin government's road to the Oslo Accord* (The Washington Institute
for Near East Policy: 1996) – socio-political circumstances
surrounding the Oslo Peace Process including a chapter
on Rabin's changing attitude towards the Palestinians.

Peri, Yoram (ed), *The Assassination of Yitzhak Rabin* (Stanford
University Press: 2000) – in-depth account of the rise of
the political right.

Rabin, Leah, *Rabin, Our Life, His Legacy* (G P Putnam's Son:
1997) – a personal account by his wife written shortly
after his assassination.

Rabin, Yitzhak, *The Rabin Memoirs* (expanded edition,
University of California Press: 1996) – his life in his own
words written in the late 1970s.

Savir, Uri, *The Process: 1,100 days that changed the Middle East*
(Random House: 1998) – the Oslo process and its negoti-
ations in the words of one of the chief negotiators on the
Israeli side.

Slater, Robert, *Rabin of Israel* (Robson Books: 1977; and
revised edition of 1993) – detailed biography, full of
anecdotes; published shortly after his second term as
Prime Minister and a more recent update.

Historical background and reference books

Cleveland, William E, *A History of the Modern Middle East*
(Westview Press: 1994) – wide-ranging introduction to
the major political and social developments of the countries in the Middle East.

Gresh, Alain and Vidal, Dominique, *The New A-Z of the Middle East* (I B Tauris: 2004) – a well-written and poignant Who's Who of the Middle East.

The Keesing's Guide to the Mid-East Peace Process (Cartermill International: 1996) – reference book about who did what, where and when.

Mattar, Phillip (ed), *Encyclopaedia of the Palestinians* (Facts on File Library: 2000) – compiled by renowned scholars it covers all issues and persons related to Palestine/Israel and the Palestinians.

Peretz, Don, *The Intifada* (Westview Press: 1990) – detailed account of the internal and external developments before and during the first Palestinian Intifada.

Rubenberg, Cheryl A, *The Palestinians: in search for a just peace* (Lynne Rienner Publishers, 2003) – a history of the Palestinians with chapters on Oslo and Rabin in respect to his policies.

Shlaim, Avi, *The Iron Wall: Israel and the Arab World* (Penguin Books: 2000) – important survey of the diplomatic history of the conflict.

Smith, Charles D, *Palestine and the Arab-Israeli conflict* (5th edition, Macmillan Press: 2004) – probably the best overview of the conflict which explores and includes the latest material and contested issues with excellent references to further reading.

Tessler, Mark, *A History of the Israeli-Palestine Conflict* (Indiana University Press: 1994) – one of the best and most detailed histories to date, covering Jewish as well as Arab and Palestinian history from their respective beginnings.

Index of Names